The Ouija Board Jurors
Mystery, Mischief and Misery
in the Jury System

Jeremy Gans

≈ WATERSIDE PRESS

The Ouija Board Jurors: Mystery, Mischief and Misery in the Jury System
Jeremy Gans

ISBN 978-1-909976-48-1 (Paperback)
ISBN 978-1-910979-39-6 (Epub E-book)
ISBN 978-1-910979-40-2 (Adobe E-book)

Copyright © 2017 This work is the copyright of Jeremy Gans. All intellectual property and associated rights are hereby asserted and reserved by the author in full compliance with UK, European and international law. No part of this book may be copied, reproduced, stored in any retrieval system or transmitted in any form or by any means, including in hard copy or via the internet, without the prior written permission of the publishers to whom all such rights have been assigned worldwide.

Cover design © 2017 Waterside Press by www.gibgob.com

Printed by Lightning Source.

Main UK distributor Gardners Books, 1 Whittle Drive, Eastbourne, East Sussex, BN23 6QH. Tel: +44 (0)1323 521777; sales@gardners.com; www.gardners.com

North American distribution Ingram Book Company, One Ingram Blvd, La Vergne, TN 37086, USA. Tel: (+1) 615 793 5000; inquiry@ingramcontent.com

Cataloguing-In-Publication Data A catalogue record for this book can be obtained from the British Library.

e-book *The Ouija Board Jurors: Mystery, Mischief and Misery in the Jury System* is available as an ebook and also to subscribers of Ebrary, Ebsco, Myilibrary and Dawsonera.

Published 2017 by
Waterside Press Ltd
Sherfield Gables
Sherfield on Loddon, Hook
Hampshire RG27 0JG.

Telephone +44(0)1256 882250
Online catalogue WatersidePress.co.uk
Email enquiries@watersidepress.co.uk

Table of Contents

Copyright and publications details *ii*
About the author *vi*
Foreword *vii*

1 **A Juror's Letter** 9
       A spate of cases *10*
       The Old Ship *15*
       Holiday camp atmosphere *19*
       Arranging a reunion *23*
       Impossible conflict *27*
       The shadow of injustice *31*

2 **Flash Harry** 35
       Larger-than-life *36*
       Blackmans Cottage *39*
       Prime suspect *43*
       Pillar of the community *46*
       English rose *50*
       Rolls of cash *55*
       Inner circle *57*

3 **Only a Game** 59
       The talking board *61*
       The most bizarre appeal *67*
       Beyond the evidence *71*
       An awkward decision *74*
       The heart of the case *78*
       The greatest Lord Chief Justice *82*

4 Iceman 85

    Imagine the shock *86*
    Smile of a killer *89*
    The bullets I had sold *91*
    Operation Arrowhead *94*
    Ali the Baddie *99*
    As if nothing had happened *102*
    Gun cupboard *104*

5 Mansfield's Window 107

    A delicate minuet *109*
    Outside of the door *115*
    The freedom to act irresponsibly *119*
    An embarrassing situation *124*
    Horror stories *127*
    The absurdities of life *131*

6 The Horrid Part 133

    The previous jury *135*
    A little levity *138*
    Your worst nightmare *141*
    Empty shells *144*
    Channelling the victim *149*
    Each one alone *154*
    The choice *157*

7 Such a Fearful Spectre 161

    First blush *162*
    Various newspaper headlines *167*
    Strange circumstances *172*
    Earth-bound evidence *176*
    A lighter tale *181*
    Such a stupid thing *185*
    Jekyll and Hyde *189*
    The pain is still here *193*

Afterword *199*
        Formal sources *199*
        Informal sources *207*

Index *209*

About the author

Jeremy Gans is a Professor at Melbourne Law School, University of Melbourne, generally regarded as Australia's top law school. He researches on all areas of criminal justice and has had treatises published on evidence (Oxford University Press), criminal law (Cambridge University Press) and criminal process rights (Federation Press, Australia), as well as numerous academic articles, including several focussing on particular criminal cases, such as the murder of Peter Falconio and the death of Azaria Chamberlain. He is also a frequent commentator in the Australian media on criminal justice and has blogged for a range of websites.

Foreword

While backpacking in Europe in 1994, I came across several newspaper tales about derailed criminal proceedings: a visiting tourist from New York who was identified by an eyewitness as a Nazi as he sat in the public gallery of a war crimes trial, a bank robbery conviction that was overturned because the accused was named 'Rob Banks', and an English murder trial under appeal because jurors had used a Ouija board to consult one of the victims. I laughed at all three stories and filed them away as neat hypotheticals for my planned career as a criminal and evidence law teacher.

After I started teaching, I was startled to discover that at least two of these tales were true. Indeed, the least believable of the three was the subject of an official law report. The English Court of Appeal ruling allowing Stephen Young's appeal against his convictions even included a transcript of the séance with murder victim Harry Fuller, courtesy of an affidavit by one of the four jurors who met in a hotel room and created a mock Ouija board with a glass and some paper. A footnote to the report pointed out that Young was convicted again at his Old Bailey retrial.

The Ouija board case has had a lengthy afterlife as an anecdote in legal judgements, articles and speeches, both in England and in my own Australia. As I write this Foreword, it featured once again in the 35th Blackstone Lecture by Court of Appeal judge Heather Hallett, 23 years after the Ouija board incident. After detailing the contemporary scourge of jurors' Googling, she adds:

> Then of course there is the jury that goes off on an inexplicable frolic of its own. In the trial of *R v Young* the charge was murder and it was in the days when juries were on occasion sent off to a hotel, for fear they may succumb to outside pressure at a crucial time in their deliberations.

While, as here, the tale is often told with a mix of humour and disbelief, sometimes anger enters the mix. The genesis of this book came in early 2014, close to the incident's 20th anniversary, when Australia's High Court, ruling on the limits to jury secrecy, described the Ouija board case as about 'irresponsible behaviour in relation to the consideration of the guilt of the accused'. Although I had long used the case as an anecdote of my own, that description just didn't sit right with my own (second-hand) experience of how heavy jurors' responsibilities were and how seriously they took them.

I had by then come to realise that official law reports are a poor window into reality. While the facts in those reports are (nearly always) true enough, they are also (nearly always) incomplete — often very incomplete. Even a little research on the Ouija board case showed that there was much more in the public domain about it than is set out in the 1994 law report, much less the anecdotes that describe or (nearly always) mis-describe it. It helps that the trial the jurors sat on involved a fairly high profile prosecution and one where the defendant continues to maintain his innocence.

As I looked further, I began to wonder: was the Ouija board incident, arguably the nadir of reported juror misbehaviour in the 20th-century, really as bad, or even as funny, as everyone (including me) had long assumed? Rather, I came to see that, far from it being, as Heather Hallett recently declared, 'inexplicable', it is at least partially understandable, once the full facts of the case before the jury, and especially the particularly distressing evidence they had to consider, are known.

My study of the case, outlined in this book, is based almost entirely on publicly available documents. The afterword outlines the particular sources I used, as well as several that I couldn't or didn't.

CHAPTER 1

A Juror's Letter

> A spate of cases — *The Old Ship* — Holiday camp atmosphere — Arranging a reunion — Impossible conflict — The shadow of injustice.

On Tuesday 19th April 1994, the Crown Court in Lewes, the administrative centre of East Sussex, received a letter that sparked six months of anguished hearings before England's Court of Appeal, a retrial and much derision of the jury system. The unsigned, handwritten, three-page letter was dated the previous day and concerned events four weeks earlier. Attached to it was a request from a man found guilty of murder by (amongst other members of his jury) the letter's author to have his conviction and twin life sentences set aside, possibly forever.

Although it was never published, the letter's content is clear from a lengthy article that appeared in the *News of the World* that Sunday. The two-page spread commenced:

> The murder trial jurors who used a ouija board before reaching their verdict held the séance after a bawdy booze-up, says the colleague who blew the whistle on them.

The tabloid's headline — 'BOOZE, DIRTY JOKES AND THEN THE OUIJA BOARD' — somehow gave an entirely sex-free case a sexy angle — apparently, in-between drinks at the bar and talk of séances at dinner, the jurors told some off-colour jokes. That was the least of their alleged sins.

The rest of the article was much more downbeat, laying out the sombre words of the juror who penned the letter:

> I just couldn't live with myself. To me, this was a miscarriage of justice. I thought to myself 'This is someone's life we're dealing with'. I was astonished that these grown-up people had played this child's game.

Juror Adrian's account of events at Brighton's *The Old Ship Hotel*—the first of many versions of the tale of the Ouija board jurors—is necessarily incomplete. He had only second-hand knowledge of the key events that night. Doubtless, his account reflects both his own slant and the editing of News Corporations's journalists and lawyers. Nevertheless, it was the first version of the story to reach the public and the courts, laying-out a tale that is troubling both in its startling centrepiece in a Brighton hotel room and the more mundane minutiae of life on a jury.

A spate of cases

> I couldn't have lived with myself that someone had been put away because of a ouija board. It has now eased my mind making a statement. I know I have made the right decision.

Whenever jurors speak out about their experiences, they make judges anxious, not only because of what they might say, but why they choose to say it. One of the courts' fears is false tales. Five weeks before the letter reached Lewes Crown Court, a different judge received an envelope in the mail. The typed letter inside alleged that another jury may have been bribed:

> Dear Sir, I was on the jury in the case of Mr Bowles, Mr Henery and a young girl. I was approached outside the court by a women who said that if I voted not guilty for Bowles and guilty for the solicitor and the girl, I would be paid £5,000. I never got any money. I think other people on the

jury may have been told this because I don't see how half of us found him not guilty after hearing the interview with the police. I am very sorry and have been having sleepless nights.

The letter bore no name or signature, and a fingerprint on the envelope could not be linked to any of the jurors or defendants. All involved in the trial denied writing the note or being offered (or offering) a bribe. Nevertheless, the two convicted persons—a solicitor and secretary convicted of defrauding a liquidator, while their co-accused client was acquitted—argued that their conviction was now unsafe, noting that there was nothing implicating them in the letter.

Six months later, England's then Lord Chief Justice, Lord Taylor, furiously rejected the defendants' argument:

> This is all total speculation. We are being invited to say that because the letter, coming from one knows not where, arrives at the court after a verdict which follows a month-long trial, there is sufficient material to justify the court in feeling such anxiety as to set the verdict aside and require a third trial, perhaps, to take place of this somewhat convoluted matter. We are unanimous in our view that that cannot be right. This letter could have been written by anybody.
>
> If a letter of this kind, unattributed either in its content or on investigation afterwards, could be sent to the court with the effect that this court will immediately set aside the jury's verdicts, one has the gravest apprehension as to when there would ever be an end to criminal trials. It would be the easiest thing for someone, not necessarily the defendants, but perhaps persons well-disposed towards them, once they have been convicted, to send anonymously a letter of this kind, and by that simple device require the court to order a retrial. The proposition has only to be stated for its absurdity to be obvious.

While the letter sent to Lewes Crown Court was similarly unsigned, its author's actual identity was revealed by the *News of the World*:

Jobless Adrian, a former factory hand, was the youngest member of the jury at Hove Crown Court in Sussex.

The tabloid even published a picture of Adrian—a nondescript young man wearing a denim jacket—superimposed on an image of hands resting on a glass tumbler surrounded by pieces of paper.

A second fear held by courts is about jurors who regret their verdict and later seek to undermine it. Two months after Adrian's letter was sent, a man convicted of a violent crowbar attack asked the Court of Appeal to investigate a letter known to have been sent by a particular juror in early-December 1993, in the handful of days between the verdict and the sentence. The juror's letter was never published, but a later summary said that

> …although she and one other member of the jury, which by that time had consisted of eleven persons, had had grave doubts about Mr Kerry's guilt, she nevertheless, in the end, had agreed with the verdict of guilty because she had felt that she was under pressure. The pressure was caused by her realisation because a failure to have agreed would possibly have resulted in the jury having to stay overnight and otherwise would have resulted in inconvenience and expense.

While there is no doubt that this letter was genuine, Lord Justice Taylor refused to order an investigation, predicting that doing so would prompt:

> …a spate of cases of jurors, perhaps the minority where there has been a majority verdict, raising questions about how the verdict was reached. Accordingly, we refuse to grant the application that any approach should be made to any of the jurors in this case. Indeed, not only do we refuse that, but we order that no approach should be made.

As it happens, a year later, a different bench of the Court of Appeal allowed the crowbar defendant's appeal because of flaws in the identification evidence used to convict him and doubts about the crucial testimony of a co-accused's girlfriend. Although they again dismissed the significance of the juror's letter, the three judges ultimately agreed with her that the conviction was unsafe.

An important difference in the Ouija board case is that Adrian apparently never expressed any doubts about the actual guilt of the man his jury convicted. Instead, his concern was the behaviour of his fellow jurors. According to the *News of the World*, he spent the weeks after the verdict 'lying awake at night thinking about it' and 'even dreaming about Harry Fuller', the victim supposedly contacted in the séance. After a talk with his parents, he consulted the Citizens Advice Bureau who advised him: 'See a solicitor and think it over'. But he had trouble finding a solicitor who wanted to help him, with three telling the former juror they couldn't assist (perhaps because English law seemed to say that such disclosures of what jurors said was illegal). The tale might have ended there, but by then word of the alleged events in the hotel had reached at least 18 people: the 12 jurors, Adrian's parents, a volunteer at the CAB and three solicitors. In the end, a fourth solicitor 'agreed to listen' to him and was left 'astonished and speechless'.

A third fear about claims of juror misconduct is that there may be no satisfactory way to respond to even genuine and serious allegations. The only other case in 1994 where the Court of Appeal ordered an investigation into a juror was sparked, not by a letter, but an event inside the courtroom. One day during his late-1993 trial, a defendant charged with trying to kill two brothers suddenly banged on the glass wall of his dock. He told his counsel that he had just seen a woman in the well of the court nodding to one of the jurors, who nodded back. After sending the jury out, the trial judge identified the woman as the sister of the two victims and asked her to leave. He then recalled the jury and asked them about the woman. After they all denied knowing her, he allowed the trial to continue. However, a friend of the defendant later attended the court and said that he recognised the juror (now the foreperson) who the victims' sister had allegedly signalled. She was a neighbour of both himself and the victims' family.

The defendant's solicitor later told the court:

> This morning I took a statement at 11 o'clock from a man called Patrick Fogarty who is a neighbour of the foreman of the jury. He became aware of this case because the babysitter, Elaine—I do not know what her second name is, she will not tell us—visited the Fogarty household two or three days ago which apparently is a regular occurrence because she speaks to Mr Fogarty's wife, Frances. She told Mr Fogarty about the case and said that Elva—that is the name of the jury foreman—had been telling her about the case and, in particular, three or four days ago indicated that eight of the jury thought he was guilty but four of the jurors thought he was innocent.

The jurors were already deliberating by then, so the trial judge refused to intervene. However, after the defendants were convicted by a 10-2 majority verdict—and less than a fortnight after Adrian's letter was received—the Lord Chief Justice told the Crown Prosecution Service to interview Elva, the jury foreperson.

The case's eventual outcome was unsatisfactory in several ways. The appeal was not heard for a further eight months, prompting the Court of Appeal to fret that 'the conduct complained of'—which was now said to include 'eye-narrowing' as well as nods—'has been added to, in the minds and memories of these witnesses, between the afternoon in question and the hearing before us.' As well, the judges were shocked to learn that the defendant's solicitor had sent two employees to interview 'Elaine', the foreperson's babysitter, while the jury was deliberating:

> Such a visit should not have been made prior to the jury returning their verdicts. The decision to organise such a visit was totally misconceived. That must be stressed in the light of the proposed change in the law which will allow jurors to return to their own homes following their retirement if their deliberations run over into another day. One of the reasons for deprecating the making of such a visit is that it is potentially damaging to an accused person because a juror or jurors or others may come to believe that an accused person is trying to pervert the course of justice by improperly affecting a juror's view.

In the end, the juror and the sister both denied on oath either signalling or knowing one another. The Court of Appeal accepted their testimony and dismissed the appeal. This conclusion leaves unexplained the coincidence that the 'signalling' that the accused and others said they saw happened to involve two women with connections to the victims' family. Nor does it respond to Fogarty's claim that the jury's foreperson apparently revealed confidential information about the jury's deliberations to a third party (Elaine, the babysitter).

But Adrian's allegations about his jury were not about winks and vague associations with the outside world, but very specific events that occurred amongst the jurors. On Monday 13th June 1994, the Court of Appeal granted murder defendant Stephen Young leave to argue juror misconduct, but withheld approval of any further investigation into Adrian's claims. The media were 'strongly warned' by the court 'that any approach to any juror involved in the case would result in possible contempt of court proceedings.'

The Old Ship

> We wanted to get out of the courtroom and have a nice time, which we did. We all sat together eating this three-course meal. It was soup, turkey dinner and gateau to follow.

While Stephen Young's murder trial lasted five weeks and his legal case wasn't to end for another decade, his jury was out for less than 24 hours. Fatefully, that was enough to require an overnight stay at a hotel.

The *News of the World* reported:

> Adrian said the other jurors felt they 'deserved a night out in a hotel' before making their decision. And they got their wish when they were sent to The Old Ship on Brighton seafront.

Brighton's *The Old Ship* was known as *The Ship* for at least its first 90 years. It gained its present name in 1650 when the *New Ship Inn* (now a *Hotel du Vin*) opened across the street. The next year, captain Nicholas Tettersell assisted Charles II's escape to France on his ship *Surprise*, an act that allowed him to purchase *The Old Ship* 20 years later using a pension gifted on the King's return. England's shifting shoreline cemented the wisdom of Tettersell's investment. Although the Ship was built on a side-street well back from the coastline, the gradual addition of new buildings in the direction of the sea and the swift submerging of what was once Lower Brighton in the Great Storm of 1703 left it on prime English Channel frontage and 'the leading, indeed the only, acceptable tavern' in the diminished town. Later owners benefited from changing social geography: the rising popularity in England of the seaside in general and (thanks to the patronage of the future King George IV) Brighton in particular. Last century, the hotel dodged wartime requisition in the 1940s and the IRA's attempt to kill Margaret Thatcher in the nearby *Grand Hotel* in 1984.

According to Adrian:

> The talk about ouija boards came late in the evening. We'd had quite a bit to drink and some nice food. Some were talking about their experiences with ouija boards. One person was convinced they definitely work, with three saying they had done it before.

For fans of ghosts, *The Old Ship* boasts plenty of famous past guests, including Niccolò Paganini (who played in the hotel's iconic Assembly Rooms), Lord Byron, Charles Dickens, William Makepeace Thackeray (who wrote, and set, some chapters of *Vanity Fair* there) and, for a brief period in the 1820s, a petty sessions (i.e. magistrates') court. Not long after Young's jury spent the night there, archaeologists uncovered smugglers' tunnels in its cellars. For regional court administrators looking for overnight accommodation that neither jurors nor taxpayers were likely to complain about, the hotel was attractive for different reasons. A homicide just inside East Sussex meant that Young's trial was held in Hove, a satellite (and suburb) of Brighton. By 1994, Brighton's oldest and largest hotel was no longer in the resort's top tier and hence well-suited (and no doubt quite happy) to host 14 visitors (12 members of the jury and two bailiffs) at the government's expense on a spring Tuesday.

But Young's jury was still lucky to receive their free meals and beds. Had the trial been held a year later, the jurors would have simply been sent to their respective homes for the night. As recounted by Lord Devlin some 40 years earlier, the famous practice of sequestering juries had been steadily waning throughout the 20th-century:

> As in modern times interference with jurors is negligible and generally only accidental, the law now has been able to relax the precautions which it formerly took and to rely much more upon the good sense of jurors. They are kept separate as a body while they are in the jury-box and also while they are in the jury-room considering their verdict, but except at those times they are no longer physically segregated. Until 1940 the old practice still prevailed in capital cases, that is to say, the jury was segregated throughout the whole trial from the moment they went into the box and took the oath until they were discharged. They had board and lodging at the expense of the county and were under the charge of the jury bailiff whose duty it was to see that no one communicated with them; and they were not allowed to have newspapers. Many a housewife must have been startled by the call of a policeman asking for a case of her husband's night things, for of course the name of any juryman who served on the trial was not known until he was called into the box. Under war conditions this rule was relaxed, and the relaxation has since been made permanent...

England's Juries Act 1974, enacted after capital punishment was abolished, allowed trial judges to let the jury 'separate' (from each other, that is, allowed them to go to their respective homes) at any time 'before the jury consider their verdict'. But those last six words meant that, when Adrian's jury failed to reach a conclusion on Young's guilt or innocence after their first afternoon of deliberations, the trial judge had no choice but to order their transport to a suitable hotel.

By 1994, jury hotel stays were easy fodder for the tabloids. The particular spectre raised by Adrian's account was of jurors seeking to get a free meal and board, presumably by needlessly drawing out their deliberations. But jurors who were less enthusiastic about a 'turkey dinner' and 'jokey evening' away from their families (or who wanted to get home to watch Whoopi Goldberg host the 66th Academy Awards, which were broadcast on British television that Tuesday night) faced an equally perverse incentive to rush their deliberations. As Young's jurors deliberated (and drank and joked and talked of ghosts), the Criminal Justice and Public Order Bill was already working its way through the UK Parliament. That controversial bill, introduced two months earlier, received plenty of scrutiny in the media and Parliament, but a minor provision expressly permitting a trial judge to separate a jury while it was deliberating went unmentioned throughout the parliamentary debate.

It is easy to see why sequestering jurors while they deliberate switched from norm to exception without protest by the end of 1994. The problems Devlin described in 1956 — rising costs and falling risks of corruption — were even more apparent in the 1990s, as lengthier and more complex trials made short jury deliberations a rarity. As well, social changes were making overnight segregation more of a burden for jurors (and, indirectly, their keepers and trial judges). A telling example occurred a fortnight before Adrian's jury stayed at *The Old Ship*. After a two-week trial concerning a complex sting aimed at Pakistani heroin traffickers, the deliberating jury was sent to Birmingham's *Royal Angus Hotel*. The next morning, a bailiff discovered that one of the jurors had placed two calls from her room's phone. The officer immediately separated her from the others and the trial judge told the court's chief clerk to question her. The upset juror explained that she had called her family about a sick child and gave the clerk the number, which the clerk called and checked against the hotel's records. He then spoke to both trial counsel, who said that they had no concerns.

These banal events had a significant aftermath. Appealing their convictions, the defendants complained about the judge's approach, arguing that had they known of further facts — that one of the calls was made at 1.28 am, that the juror was actually the foreperson, and that 'she was from the Asian community' — they would have pursued the matter further.

The Court of Appeal pronounced both the juror's phone calls and the trial judge's informal response 'irregular'. However:

> ...we are satisfied that there is no valid reason in this case to impugn the explanation given by the juror concerned, and we are satisfied that had the judge adopted the correct procedure, he would have come to the same conclusion, namely, that there was no prejudice to the accused, and would in the result have taken the same course as he did.

But the Ouija board case was not the only appeal that year showcasing a further worry: that the benefits of separating jurors from the outside world may be outweighed by the costs of leaving them in contact with each other away from the court's watchful eye.

Holiday camp atmosphere

> One of the jury produced two pieces of paper and started talking about the previous night. I overheard, and at first I couldn't believe it. They had secretly gone to one of their rooms and gone through with it.

Adrian's sole experiences with his jury were as part of a group of 12 (or 14, including the two bailiffs at the hotel). When talk of séances came up at dinner:

> I was interested to hear what they said, but found it funny. Those who had done it before were laughing about it, but those who hadn't were quite serious. We had a curfew of 11 pm and had to be in our rooms before then. I went ten minutes early because I'd had three pints and was a bit tipsy. Another woman had a headache and went to bed early. I didn't get a good night's sleep, because I'd drunk too much and felt a bit rough and the bed wasn't too comfortable.

While *The Old Ship* probably didn't appreciate this review of its beds, Adrian had no doubt what the real problem was that night. As the *News of the World*'s headline emphasised, the evening had been anything but sober:

> Everyone had a few to drink and we were laughing at the girls who had too much. There was a real holiday camp atmosphere. We really needed to relax because the trial had gone on so long. There were a couple of dirty jokes told and everyone was in a good mood.

He added: 'What went wrong, I think, was that a few beers came into it and mouths started talking'.

This certainly wasn't the first time that alcohol, hotels and jurors were said to be a bad mix. Famously, over a hundred years earlier, the trial of farmer Francis Hynes for an alleged sectarian killing in Ireland was the subject of complaints, not only of judicial bias and jury packing, but also hotel misconduct, sourced from a hotel resident (and politician) in a letter to *The Freeman*:

> Dear Sir,—I think the public ought to be made aware of the following facts. The jury in the murder case of the Queen v. Hynes were last night 'locked up,' as it is termed, for the night at the Imperial Hotel, where I also was staying. I was awakened from sleep shortly after midnight by the sounds of a drunken chorus, succeeded after a time by scuffling, rushing, coarse laughter, and horse-play along the corridor on which my bedroom opens. A number of men, it seemed to me, were falling about the passage in a maudlin state of drunkenness, playing ribald jokes. I listened with patience for a considerable time, when the door of my bedroom was burst open, and a man whom I can identify (for he carried a candle unsteadily in his hand) staggered in, plainly under the influence of drink, hiccuping, 'Hallo, old fellow, all alone?' My answer was of a character that induced him to bolt out of the room in as disordered a manner as he had entered. Having rung the bell, I ascertained that these disorderly persons were jurors in the case of the Queen v. Hynes, and that the servants of the hotel had been endeavouring in vain to bring them to a sense of their misconduct. I thought it right to

convey to them a warning that the public would hear of their proceedings. The disturbance then ceased. It is fair to add that no more than three or four men appeared to be engaged in the roaring and in the tipsy horse-play that followed. I leave the public to judge the loathsomeness of such a scene upon the night when these men held the issues of life and death for a young man in the flower of youth—when they had already heard evidence which, if unrebutted, they must have known would send him to a felon's grave. The facts I am ready to support upon oath.

After Hynes was convicted of murder, he penned a lengthy poem on the eve of his execution that included the line 'A Dublin Orange jury on that Memorial Day, mad drunk and blind with fury, they swore my life away'. The jury foreman, in his own letter to the editor, blamed the whole incident on a single drunken juror, prompting the trial judge to imprison the newspaper's editor for three months for contempt of court.

By the time of the Ouija board case, diligent jurors were worrying the Court of Appeal more than drunken ones. The only other English verdict overturned for juror misconduct in 1994 was a doctor's conviction for defrauding the National Health Service. The complex trial, where the defendant insisted that he had just muddled his paperwork, stretched for 25 days in mid-1992 and, after two days of deliberations, the jury was invited to reach a majority verdict. When the trial judge asked whether the jurors wanted to continue deliberating or retire for the night, the foreperson asked if they could take a copy of some of the case documents to their hotel. After counsel worried that the jury might continue their deliberations away from the court, the judge observed that she couldn't stop them but would try, eventually telling them that 'it seems to me that you would be much better advised to put the whole thing out of your mind, if you can, for this evening'. But then the transcript records her saying:

> I see some of you are shaking your heads. I think if you must discuss it, ladies and gentlemen, it must be in private and it is not easy to arrange in a hotel if you want to go on talking about it. With some reluctance, I will do this if you want to…

The next morning the jury took just 40 minutes to reach a majority verdict.

Two years later, after finding that the jury had obviously deliberated at their hotel, the Court of Appeal said:

> The dangers inherent in deliberations continuing in a hotel, which have been canvassed in the course of this hearing, are obvious. Unless the jurors are all together in one room, rival camps may be formed. If a jury is divided then obviously some are taking one view and the remainder are taking the other view. There is a clear danger that pressure may be brought to bear on individual jurors in the opposite camp at a time when they are not acting as a collegiate body.
>
> One of the strengths of the jury system is that they do act as a body, and if there is disagreement then individual jurors can look to others of the same view for support. If they continue their discussions outside the jury room, then those of a weaker disposition may be open to persuasion without having the support of others of the same mind.

The Court of Appeal allowed the appeal, pronouncing the course of events a 'serious irregularity'. It delivered that ruling on Friday 21st October 1994, three days before a different bench ruled on the Ouija board case.

It would be naïve to think that the four jurors at *The Old Ship* were the first or last to secretly meet up in one of their rooms after lights out. Human nature suggests the rule that what happens in a juror hotel room stays in that hotel room. Indeed, one of the hotel room jurors would later describe the evening's events ending when 'we retired to our rooms and agreed not to relate what we'd done to anyone'. Had that vow been kept, the story would have ended there. But it wasn't:

> I didn't think anything else about ouija boards until the next morning, when it was raised again half-way through breakfast. The 12 of us on the jury and the two court bailiffs were sitting round a long table.

In line with the Court of Appeal's fears, the breakfast conversation apparently did not include the 'jury as a whole'. Adrian merely 'overheard' another juror's account:

> He just came out with it and said: 'We've done a ouija board and got in contact with Harry and Nicola.' He said he and three female jurors went to one of their rooms. They'd had a few drinks and just decided to do it.

The two bailiffs either didn't care or (as they later told the Court of Appeal) didn't hear:

> We should add that more than one juror admitted on affidavit to having had more drink than was good for them whilst in the hotel and to feeling the worse for it the next morning. Neither of the bailiffs, according to their affidavits, seemed to have been aware of that or of the fact that four jurors had got together in one room over an ouija board.

Adrian didn't care at first either. He 'was lost for words and couldn't stop laughing—but I could see they were all taking this seriously'.

Arranging a reunion

> The jurors seemed honest people. We were a mixture—housewives, shop workers, self-employed businessmen, a plumber, retired bank manager and insurance broker.

There is little public information about the jury who stayed at *The Old Ship*. During the trial, the press duly reported that the jury had an equal number of men and women. 'Jobless' Adrian's brief list of the other jurors' occupations reveals little, except for the minor oddity that Stephen Young was tried and found guilty by a fellow insurance broker. Putting aside Adrian and the hotel room quartet, that leaves four men and three women with no alleged role in the events, except for mealtime conversations in the bailiffs' presence.

At the case's first hearing at the Court of Appeal, the immediate issue was who exactly the judges were being asked to investigate:

THE LORD CHIEF JUSTICE: If we allow this matter to go further, what evidence would you wish to seek? Presumably, Mr Penry-Davey, you would wish an affidavit from the person from whom there is only an unsigned statement?

MR PENRY-DAVEY : Yes.

THE LORD CHIEF JUSTICE : Which the court would probably have to confine itself to ordering that it should cover whether the board was or was not used in the hotel; what was said at breakfast; and how it all came to be known. The chain of information contained in the solicitor's letter is something about which we should like to know more. Also the foreman of the jury and the two jury bailiffs, from whom we have statements, but they may not include everything. Would that about cover it?

Young's counsel, David Penry-Davey, was happy with the court's proposal 'at that stage'.

Penry-Davey, then aged 52, had been at the bar for 29 years at that point, and a Queen's Counsel for the previous six. The following year, he was elected vice-chairman of England's Bar Council and proceeded in 1997 to the chairmanship, where he championed the then controversial role of juries in trials of complex fraud, Penry-Davey's speciality: 'My experience over many years tells me that generally they've got it right and I can't see the prospect of any alternative improving on that record'. *The Independent* described him as 'tall' and 'avuncular', a former Bar golf champion, and, as a graduate of a grammar school and King's College London, a living rebuttal of complaints of elitism in the Bar. (On the other hand, the article conceded, there was his 'double-barrelled name' and his support of wigs). A knighthood and judicial appointment soon followed his chairmanship of the bar, and then brief fame when he was attacked by a gang *en route* to the Old Bailey:

> The judge's spectacles were smashed as the youths tried to kick him to the ground. As they made off with his wallet, mobile phone and diary, he ran up the station steps and jumped into the car of a bemused driver sitting at traffic lights. When the youths realised they were being followed they threw away his possessions and split up.

Mr Justice Penry-Davey recovered his wallet and phone and went straight to court, delivering a judgement (refusing a bid for release by the killers of toddler James Bulger) with a black eye. Known for his 'loud' shirts and socks, he was diagnosed a year later with Parkinson's disease, but stayed on the bench for a further eight years. His obituary in 2015 observed that 'he was defence counsel for an alleged murderer where his submissions left the jury in such a quandary that they used a Ouija board to try to contact the victim for guidance'.

Penry-Davey's opponent at Young's trial and appeal also eventually ended up on the bench. Prosecutor Michael Lawson began his career as a barrister five years after Penry-Davey, but he took silk a year ahead of him and was active on the Bar Council for three years, including as president of its South-East Circuit. A champion of diversity and equity, he volunteered to be the defendant in an unsuccessful action by a junior barrister to establish a minimum wage for Bar pupils. From the Circuit Court bench (where he was appointed a decade after Penry-Davey), he named one exception to his praise of his colleagues:

> There is, however, one area where the Bar has failed to take sufficiently seriously the repeated warnings in relation to the continued use of juries in the longer cases. The Bar, including those who practise in the criminal courts, whilst insisting on the preservation of juries in all crown court trials, have singularly failed to reduce the length of any class of trial to a significant degree.

Eventually, Judge Lawson sat on the court Adrian wrote to, Lewes Crown Court, where he received national attention for his stern stance on teacher Jeremy Forrest, who he sentenced to five years in prison for taking a 15-year-old student to France to hide their sexual relationship. Lawson retired in 2016, after eleven years as a judge.

At Young's appeal, Lawson disagreed with his opponent that a small investigation into the jury would suffice:

> My Lord, the matter is of importance, as your Lordship says. If your Lordships come to a certain view, then it must be that all the parties involved in the case should be questioned within the limits of what has been submitted. It would be quite wrong to do it in piecemeal fashion, we submit, but the matter is of sufficient importance that we submit that your Lordships' decision should be arrived at before we discuss the extent of any inquiry that should be made.

When the Lord Chief Justice pressed his proposal for a limited inquiry at the next hearing, the defence argued that at least the other three jurors in the hotel room should also be questioned, perhaps worrying that one or more of them would downplay the events of the evening. In turn, the prosecution, maybe keen to show that the problem did not affect the whole jury, now said that all the jurors should be questioned:

> Once one takes the step of not receiving information formally from the foreman, which is often what has tended to have happened, once one goes further and a formal investigation is undertaken, I respectfully submit that each juror should be approached...

The defence agreed, leaving the Court of Appeal with little choice. On 23rd June 1994, it ruled:

> We propose to direct that affidavits should be obtained from all the jurors and from the two bailiffs, and there should be investigation of the matters contained in the letter of 18 April from solicitors to the Lewes Crown Court.

Adrian told the *News of the World* that his jury had parted amicably four weeks earlier:

> They were even arranging a reunion a year after the case but I doubt I'll be going to it now. I think it will be in my mind to keep out of their way.

Whether or not they were aware by then of Adrian's actions, all of the jurors would now be drawn into a reunion of sorts, nine months earlier than they had planned.

Impossible conflict

> We'd gone back to the court by coach and got there by 10 o'clock. The verdict came before noon and I glimpsed Young as he was shaking his head. His wife was crying and there was a big roar from the public gallery. Then I saw the seriousness of it all.

Within moments of pronouncing Stephen Young guilty of murder, Adrian 'felt really guilty' himself:

> The women on the jury started crying. I think they realised how serious it was. I felt distressed putting someone away for life — it's a hard thing on your mind. It was on my conscience. I thought I should have said something at the time, but because of my age I wasn't taken seriously.

If Adrian had spoken out at the time, the trial judge could probably have questioned the jurors himself about what happened at *The Old Ship* (or asked his officers to do so). But, with the trial long over, the jury dismissed and the matter in the hands of an appeal court with largely administrative staff, the Lord Chief Justice needed to innovate.

A month earlier, when the allegation was that the jury foreperson knew a relative of the victims, the Lord Chief Justice simply asked the

Crown Prosecution Service to interview the pair. However, the Crown scotched that idea in Stephen Young's appeal:

> I respectfully submit that it is not appropriate either for an officer involved in the investigation or a member of the Crown Prosecution Service in the case or the defendant's solicitor to have anything to do with the investigation. It should be done, in my submission, by a solicitor appointed by your Lordship.

This stance is sensible. The Crown was a party to the appeal and had already put submissions in favour of dismissing Young's complaint, so Young could scarcely be expected to trust the prosecution to investigate the jurors properly. At the same time, it would be wrong for Young's solicitor to speak to them, as they had recently found his client guilty.

At an earlier hearing, a third barrister, Dorian Lovell-Pank, was briefed by the Treasury Solicitor (the government's legal service) to appear as a 'friend of the court', assisting the judges on legal issues. At 48, Lovell-Pank was slightly younger than the other barristers, having only become a Queen's Counsel a year earlier. Although his main experience was in prosecuting, he was about to pivot to defending and his later career would include trials in Gibraltar—he was a fluent Spanish speaker, having grown up in Buenos Aires—and involvement in Russia's revived jury system. Although Lovell-Pank's role assisting the court ended with the earlier hearing, he had nevertheless presented himself before the Court of Appeal 'as a matter of courtesy' because he was involved in a hearing in the courtroom next door:

> THE LORD CHIEF JUSTICE: Yes, thank you. Mr Lovell-Pank, even before counsel for the Crown said what he did, we were beginning to wonder whether it might be best if the Treasury Solicitor were to take this on.
>
> MR LOVELL-PANK: Bearing in mind that I was instructed as amicus, strictly speaking I was not acting on behalf of the Treasury Solicitor. I was instructed to assist the court in whatever way I could. I should have thought,

subject to taking proper instructions about it, that the Treasury Solicitor might carry out that investigation, but I would need to take instructions.

The court asked the Treasury Solicitor to investigate the jurors, subject to its raising any objections.

Lovell-Pank immediately lived-up to his reputed eye for detail, asking that transcripts of the hearings to date be provided to any investigators and suggesting that any police officer assisting be of the rank of 'not less than' chief inspector, with no connection to the Sussex police. More perceptively, he raised the awkward position the jurors themselves would face:

> Your Lordship will recall that in the course of the discussion last Monday the suggestion was floated, but then died a natural death, that the use of a ouija board within a jury room could, in certain circumstances, be an act tending to pervert the course of justice. It could be; it is a matter for discussion. If a juror who was alive to the issue, or on the ball (if I can use that expression)—if he was on the ball and a Superintendent arrived at his house, he might want to take advice, and he might be told that he must not say anything which might incriminate him.

As a formal matter, the Court of Appeal was investigating Young's murder conviction. But, given Young's complaint, it was really the jurors themselves (or at least some of them) who were under investigation. Much like criminal suspects, they would be contacted at their homes and then questioned by a senior police officer about their conduct, which was alleged to be potentially criminal.

Indeed, jurors can be prosecuted for their trial behaviour. A startling example occurred in Canada a year after Young's appeal. Participants in an eight-month Vancouver murder trial noticed a juror, Gillian Guess, 'flip[ping] her hair and look[ing] seductive' towards one defendant. After the jury acquitted all of the accused, the police pursued their suspicions by tapping Guess's phone, eventually discovering that the pair had been sleeping together throughout the trial. Guess was convicted of attempting to pervert the course of justice and both she and the defendant were sentenced to prison, in her case for 18 months, even though no-one claimed that she reached a false verdict. British Columbia's highest court rejected her appeal:

> That the appellant well knew what she was doing in carrying on an affair with an accused was not in accord with her duties as a juror is clear from the evidence. She was secretive about the matter and in discussions with her sister and friends she acknowledged that what was occurring was wrong. She observed that she felt 'conflicted'. That, of course, precisely identifies the difficulty–she was in a position of impossible conflict. Would this conduct have a tendency to pervert or obstruct the course of justice? The answer to this question is obviously in the affirmative. The juror would be privy knowingly or unknowingly to information not possessed by other jurors and because of the emotional ties between her and the accused would be hampered in properly performing the impartial functions of a judicial officer.

The four hotel room jurors were also (briefly) 'secretive about the matter' and, as will be seen, they acknowledged (amongst themselves) that they 'had gone too far', were 'privy... to information [of a sort] not possessed by other jurors' and (in some cases) became 'emotional'. So, a conviction for attempting to pervert the course of justice couldn't be ruled out, had any of them been prosecuted. The upshot is that at least some of the jurors would indeed have been well-advised to refuse to participate in the investigation, unless they were promised immunity from prosecution.

The Lord Chief Justice's response was that his court would cross this bridge if it came to it:

> Mr Lovell-Pank it has been helpful of you to draw attention to that possibility. Our view is that if problems arise of that kind, we will have to deal with them as and when, but for the moment we propose to direct that affidavits should be obtained from all the jurors and from the two bailiffs, and there should be investigation of the matters contained in the letter of 18 April from solicitors to the Lewes Crown Court, only so far as the matters

in that letter relate to how the allegation of the irregularity arose and how it was communicated.

He also postponed the question of the jurors themselves being asked to testify:

> I think what we ought to do, so far as attendance of witnesses is concerned, is to see the affidavits when they are prepared. If those can be produced to the court, then the court can indicate which witnesses ought to attend the hearing, if any, with a view possibly to being called. If a witness cannot contribute anything, there is no point in having them all come. We should like to see the fruits of the inquiry on paper in affidavit form, and then decide which witnesses ought to attend.

As it happens, none of these contingencies arose. The Treasury Solicitor accepted its assigned role, a suitable senior police officer was found, the jurors all agreed to be interviewed and none were either called as witnesses or charged as criminals.

The shadow of injustice

> I still feel bad about it, but I'm glad I've done what I think is right. It's not that I wanted to snitch on other jury members, who were nice people, but in the interests of justice all this had to come out.

The decision to ask all 12 jurors what they knew about events at the hotel was risky. An example of how such an inquiry can go awry has since played out. In 2014, Australia's High Court told a lower court to investigate a note that was handed to a bailiff after a jury verdict. The note said: 'I have been physically coerced by a fellow juror to change my plea to be aligned with the majority vote'. The High Court glibly forecast a simple investigation:

The Ouija Board Jurors

Any doubt or ambiguity as to the true meaning of the note might be resolved relatively easily by inquiry of the juror who made the note. An inquiry may reveal, either that the 'physical coercion' referred to in the note was no more than robust debate, or that whatever pressure was described, it had, in truth, no real effect upon the decision of the juror who wrote the note…[I]t cannot be assumed that the inquiry would be 'wide-ranging and intrusive…into the deliberations of the jury, [involving] the interrogation of all 12 members of the jury'.

The inquiry took the better part of two years. The lower court first struggled to locate the juror who wrote the note and then to convince (and ultimately compel) him to explain it. When the juror (who turned out to be the foreperson) finally spoke, he said that he was indeed assaulted by another juror to make him change his vote. In the end, all 12 jurors testified in person before the appeal court. Their accounts varied on all manner of details, from the sequence and length of deliberations, to how and when the foreperson left the discussion, the layout of the toilets where the assault was said to have occurred, and even whether or not the lead prosecutor was blind. Ultimately, the appeal court found that there was no coercion, because there was little or no support for the foreperson's claims of hostility in the jury room or any opportunity for such an assault in the toilets. 'The shadow of injustice has been dispelled', the court declared, and 'the integrity of the verdict has been put beyond question'. Not all who read the jurors' accounts of the chaotic deliberations would agree.

For all its many oddities, the Ouija board case did not suffer this fate. The Court of Appeal's investigation broadly confirmed what Adrian told the *News of the World*. In its eventual judgement on Young's appeal, the Court of Appeal reported:

> In the result, we obtained affidavits from all 12 jurors and from the two bailiffs. The affidavits were provided to the parties although the names of the jurors (save for the four who were alleged to have been involved with the ouija board at the hotel) were not disclosed, numbers being substituted instead. We also received an affidavit from the appellant's solicitor

describing how the matter raised on the appeal came to his attention. Whilst there were differences of detail, the affidavits gave a reasonably clear and consistent account of what occurred in the hotel.

The affidavit of one of those jurors, partly set out in the court's judgement, continues the story of the Ouija board case.

CHAPTER 2

Flash Harry

Larger-than-life — Blackmans Cottage — Prime suspect — Pillar of the community — English rose — Wads of cash — Inner circle

Sometime after 11 pm on Tuesday 22nd March 1994, four fingers were placed on an upturned hotel room glass. Those present included Ray, the elected foreperson of Stephen Young's jury and also the quartet's informal leader. Ray was experienced with Ouija boards, while the other three jurors were Ouija virgins. It was Ray who tore a sheet of paper into 28 pieces, labelled them with 'yes', 'no' and the letters of the alphabet and arranged them in a circle around the glass. It was also Ray who got the séance rolling, voicing questions into the air.

Ouija boards, like juries, operate on the basis of consensus — the consent of all, or at least a clear majority — of those around the table. Each time Ray asked 'Is anyone there?', the answer was in the hands — well, the forefingers — of everyone touching the glass. Whatever it was that caused the tumbler to move in response — the jurors' subconscious twitches, the foreperson's pushy forefinger, a passing ghost — could be readily countered by any of them. Had the glass stayed still, roamed the table at random or simply tipped over, the verdict the jury delivered the next morning would still have been standing eight months later. If the tumbler had moved to 'no', then the evening would probably have ended in laughter, instead of tears. But, as the Lord Chief Justice grimly reported, the 'glass went to yes' and 'the matter proceeded as follows, according to one of those present'.

The words that emerged from the jurors' makeshift Ouija board were at once shocking and banal. Having spent the past month hearing detailed testimony about a vicious and heartless crime, the four jurors spent their hotel stay's midnight hour laboriously repeating the tale's basics, letter-by-letter. The account of the glass, bits of paper and fingers was necessarily superficial, name-checking those involved and identifying the opportunity, means and motive that briefly brought them together. Just as others would in decades to come, the Ouija board naturally left out much of the case's context and complications, and added some patent nonsense into the mix. Nevertheless, its story is a convenient entrée to the questions before the jury.

Larger-than-life

> Ray said, 'Who is it?' The glass spelt out 'Harry Fuller'.

'When I say the glass spelt it out', the unnamed juror's affidavit explained, 'I mean it went to each letter'. She added: 'I realised Fuller was the subject of the evidence we were hearing'. As a recent murder victim, Harry Fuller would seem an appealing subject for a séance, but other things about him made him less ideal. For starters, as Adrian pointed out at breakfast the next morning, Harry's dyslexia meant that he 'could not read or write well'.

The day after his death, the *Kent & Sussex Courier* described Harry as 'a car dealer who also had interests in the building trade and in the property business'. More colourful descriptions of the 45-year-old followed: 'shady wheeler dealer', 'wealthy rogue', 'fly boy', 'gipsy romeo', 'conman'. A 'woman acquaintance' told *Today*:

> He was a real charmer, good looking and always joking. With his long black curly hair he was popular with the women. But we all knew he was bit of a bad lad—a rogue who had a finger in every pie going.

The papers pursued comments from his 'two ex-wives and ... string of girlfriends' but 'few people were prepared to talk about him on the record'. Harry's previous wife, Elizabeth, living with the couple's three-year-old daughter in nearby Crowborough, told them: 'It's a long time ago and I'd rather leave it all in the past'. She knew nothing of his first wife (if, indeed, she existed).

Elizabeth's neighbours were happier to unload, explaining that Harry and Elizabeth had moved to the town after a storm devastated the region in 1987. One widow described how Harry:

> ...offered to replace six slates blown off my roof and charged me £200 for it. I was a bit frightened of him so I paid up. Then he dug up my front path saying he smelt gas and there must be a leak. He went around on his hands and knees with a lighted match, found nothing and then charged me to relay the path.

The account of another retiree, who asked Harry to repair a chimney, also mixed some menace into the tale of incompetence:

> He got up there with a sledgehammer and the whole lot came through my porch and left a big hole in the top of my house. There was nothing I could do because he made me pay £800 by cheque before he did the job. He was a big bloke and I found him a bit intimidating. He was always banging about with cars. At the time he was driving a Porsche and there were always cars lined up in the street. I don't know much about him other than that. The police came round once or twice.

But the landlord of a pub Harry later frequented in Lewes remembered him more warmly as a 'larger-than-life figure'.

Harry's final neighbour, who lived above (and ran) a tearoom next door to the cottage where he died, described him as 'a bit of an Arthur Daley character'. This reference to the TV series *Minder* (then in its eleventh and final season) was and remains instantly recognisable to anyone in England. Originally a vehicle for singer and actor Dennis Waterman, it yielded a surprise hit in Arthur Daley, who employed Waterman's character as his bodyguard. George Cole's iconic used car dealer became sufficiently popular in his own right that the series survived Waterman's exit. Daley's name lives on today as an all-purpose description of a small-time businessman with mid-size shonky dealings and big-time ideas. Harry's resemblance to Cole's character extends beyond his occupation to his alleged capers:

> On one occasion he was dangled by his ankles from a balcony in Woolwich, London. The people who did it to him then drove his Porsche into the Thames.

Adding to the mild mystique, an employee of Harry's other final neighbour, a butcher's shop, said: 'Sometimes he was not here for two or three days. We don't know where he went'.

The police slowly fed the press what they knew of Harry's background:

> We have seen quite a few of Mr Fuller's business associates and we are seeing more. His line of business was car dealing, building and roofing. It seems the thing he has done most recently is car dealing. He went to auctions regularly.

Others were told: 'The victim was a bit of a rogue and he is well-known to us'. The *Daily Express* reported that one of Harry's former associates was 'in jail for manslaughter'. The car dealer had 'a number of proved and unproved charges against him', including 'convictions for dishonesty, burglary and violence'. He was a 'discharged bankrupt and in his younger days served sentences in both borstal and prison'. The *Argus* quoted anonymous women's tales about his 'compulsive lying, split personality, violent temper and love affair with money'. But others labelled him a 'loveable rogue' who told fantastic stories about himself: he'd been given a Porsche by Jack Nicholson, once played guitar in Paul McCartney's Wings, was friendly with pop star David Essex and fathered a 'love child' with Kelly McGillis (Tom Cruise's love interest in *Top Gun*). Harry also claimed to know the Kray twins, who terrorised London's East End in the mid-1960s when the car dealer would have been a teenager.

The nickname that finally stuck was 'Flash Harry', that of a character, Henry Cuthbert Evans, in the 1950s and 1960s *St Trinian's* films (and also played by George Cole). Cuthbert was a parody of bully (and later adventurer) Harry Flashman from *Tom Brown's School Days*. The *Oxford Dictionary* defines the nickname as a reference to 'an ostentatious, loudly-dressed, and usually ill-mannered man', a fair description of Harry Fuller. While Harry liked to talk about and show wads of cash, few believed his claims to be a millionaire. Harry, said the detective leading the investigation into his death,

> was an exaggerator and lived in a larger-than-life world. If he had £3,000 in his pocket he would tell you he had £30,000. If he had one Rolls-Royce, he would tell you he had five...In the end, Harry's exaggeration may have killed him.

Or perhaps 'Flash Harry' was another colourful lie. A 'business associate', Jeffrey White, later told the jury that Harry did indeed have 2.6 million pounds in a Jersey bank account in his barrister's name.

In short, Harry's own tales rendered the real Harry Fuller largely unknowable and a challenging target for interrogation via a séance.

Blackmans Cottage

> Ray said, 'Who killed you?'

When Harry Fuller died, he was facing away from whoever it was who shot him. However, the jurors had reason to think that he knew his killer. The investigation's initial chief told *Today*:

> Mr Fuller wouldn't let anyone in unless he knew them. He was very careful about who he let over the doorstep.

Jeffrey White, Harry's business associate, confirmed this on the second day of Stephen Young's trial:

> He told me had a chequered past and there may be some people who wanted to find out where he lived. He thought there may be individuals who might want to make a name for themselves by attacking him.

The car dealer 'would only open his front door after checking at the window to see who was there'. He lived in 'constant fear' and was 'preoccupied with sheltering' his new wife.

Harry's move to his final address in a village high street came five months before his death and shortly after his third marriage. Wadhurst is seven miles from both Harry's previous marital home in Crowborough and his other relatives near Royal Tunbridge Wells but is respectively a quarter and a tenth the size of those towns. They are all on the High Weald, a range running across Sussex and Kent covered in ancient woodlands and difficult soil that have kept the area relatively unpopulated compared to the rest of England's south-east. Cotchford Farm, the home of A A Milne and his son Christopher Robin and inspiration for Winnie-the-Pooh's 100 Acre Wood is ten miles to Wadhurst's west. Although nearly a thousand years old and granted the status of a 'market town' for the last 750 or so, Wadhurst has never been more than a village, with a current population of less than five thousand. The town is mostly arranged along a single street that follows one of the Weald's characteristic ridges, just within the Sussex side of the border with Kent.

Claiming that 'its normal idea of a crime wave was two drunks arrested on a Saturday night', the English media dubbed Wadhurst 'sleepy' and a 'Miss Marple village'. In a minor scandal months after Harry's death, not a single one of the town's residents attended a police 'question and answer' session held in the village hall. But Wadhurst has received more than a small village's share of big town trouble. In the early-20th century, it was the scene of several shocking murders — a son killing his widowed mother, a local labourer strangling a ten-year-old while she was picking blackberries, a mother drowning her daughter, and another mother and daughter being shot by an army deserter as they picnicked. The village lost dozens serving in World War One (including 25 in a single day), was bombed by the Luftwaffe flying to and from London during the next war and was denuded of its oak trees by the Great Storm of 1987. Nor was it free of lesser crime. After attending the failed police meeting after Harry's death, a journalist discovered someone had stolen his car; it was later found dumped in a field, 'bonnetless' and with 'a smashed steering column'.

Wadhurst's most startling encounter with the outside world occurred on 20th January 1956, when the village's high street was partly destroyed by a Meteor aeroplane. The flaming object's entirely terrestrial origin was an air force base over a hundred miles to the north. The Meteor WS 661 was well off-route on a training flight when its student pilot entered into a diving turn over his parents' home in nearby Durgate. Flying north over the village, the plane clipped something—either a tree near Wadhurst Castle or a bungalow—and became a fireball that killed both of its occupants and two Wadhurst residents (including the man whose wife and daughter were shot while picnicking two decades earlier). The resulting blaze destroyed a hotel and grocery store and left part of the town's high street a blackened ruin for years. The bland row of modern buildings that eventually rose from the ashes permanently diminished the village's character.

It was Wadhurst's modernity that most likely attracted Harry. The town supports an outsize number of schools, in part due to the destruction of a neighbouring village school in 1944 by a primitive missile. In the post-Meteor reconstruction, a former county school was relocated to a new building set back from the high street on the site of a mansion, Uplands House. Despite (or perhaps because of) massive damage during the 1987 storm and later rebuilding, Uplands Community College became a 'beacon school' with over a thousand students commuting there. One result was a large overflow carpark built next to the college's tennis courts, backing onto a line of 17th and 18th-century houses on the high street. The line of houses was in the prettiest part of the contemporary village and included a former blacksmith's, butcher's, a tea shop and a chemist's. Sandwiched in between was the three-story Blackmans Cottage. Its frontage onto a retail street may have eased Harry's security concerns, while the large car park at the rear served his business interests. A longstanding friend explained:

> Harry was always buying cars and looking for somewhere to store them. When he got the house in Wadhurst, it was like him winning the pools, because he got a free car park there for all the cars he wanted to park.

The friend had spent several hours with Harry at a car auction the day before he died: 'I asked Harry to get me a vehicle because, having bought me one before, I knew he'd get me something reasonable'.

The village itself knew nothing of Harry. A local publican said that car dealer and his wife

> came in occasionally for a drink and a bite to eat. They would just sit quietly in the corner. They had only recently moved into the village and I didn't even know their names.

The owner of a nearby gift shop said: 'Nobody really knew them. They weren't Wadhurst people'. The manager of the butcher next door could only say that he had seen the Fullers at his store from time to time. A lodger above told the press: 'We heard nothing at all last night. It was very quiet'.

Beyond the other party wall, the tea shop proprietor told the media:

> We did not know them. They only moved in about last October. They were very quiet and kept to themselves. I wouldn't expect this to happen anywhere, let alone a village like Wadhurst. I'm shocked because we live above the shop and you would have thought we'd hear a gun being fired. They were a nice polite couple who'd nod or say hello in the street, but they kept themselves very much to themselves.

But he belatedly realised that he and his wife had heard the killer's gun:

> We heard some bangs–three or four taps at about 9 am. We didn't realise what it was and turned the radio down. From what we now gather, those

bangs could have been the shots. It is a shock to realise that we might have heard somebody being killed.

Harry was last seen alive just after half past eight on a Wednesday morning, 10th February 1993. Leaving his front door ajar, he visited nearby Goble's tobacconist, on the next block of the high street, to buy the morning papers and some cigarettes, returning two minutes later.

That evening, his body was found 'sprawled in a washroom' downstairs in the cottage. He had been pulled out of sight and left propped against a washing machine, with his head under a leather coat and his torso covered in white powder, his mobile phone lying beside him. The car dealer had been shot through the back, the bullet entering next to his spine, piercing his heart and lodging in his chest. The house's doors were locked, the curtains were drawn and there was no sign of a break-in or of anything being stolen. A Wadhurst solicitor told the media: 'I knew them personally and was renting the cottage to them. This has come as a complete shock'. Blackmans Cottage, soon dubbed the 'murder house' by locals, has since been renamed 'Spring Cottage'.

Prime suspect

> The glass spelt out 'Stephen Young done it'.

Harry Fuller's last recorded words (unless you count the Ouija board) were broadcast on British television on 15th April 1993, just over two months after he died:

Caller:	How are you doing?
Harry:	Very well indeed. It couldn't be better.
Caller:	I popped over last night to see you.
Harry:	What time?
Caller:	'bout seven.
Harry:	I was at the gym, up at the, um, golf club.

Caller:	—Oh—
Harry:	At Ticehurst.
Caller:	There were some lights on but I knocked.
Harry:	Alright. See you in the morning my darling.
Caller:	My dear.
Harry:	Eight o'clock.
Caller:	Yep. Bye.
Harry:	Ciao for now.

The heavily edited recording was part of a ten-minute segment on the BBC's *Crimewatch*.

Then in its ninth year, the monthly programme features reconstructions of unsolved crimes and public appeals for information. The show had recently played a prominent role in the investigation of the death of Merseyside toddler James Bulger, who was killed two days after Harry. The mid-February edition broadcast an enhanced version of the now iconic CCTV image of two boys (thought at the time to be aged between 12 and 14) leading the two-year-old out of a shopping centre, prompting calls identifying the pair and the shocking detail that his killers were barely ten-years-old. The programme's April 1993 edition crammed four reconstructions as well as smaller segments into a brisk 45 minutes. The Fuller case was covered third, in between an abduction and a home invasion, followed by a reminder that violent crimes are rare and that viewers are more likely to die by accident.

Host Sue Cook introduced the Fuller reconstruction by telling viewers they would hear 'the actual voice of a man the police are desperately trying to trace'. An actor playing Harry was shown chatting on his mobile phone while driving a convertible down a wooded road and then attending the car auction with his friend. As the scene shifted to the couple in their living room and a phone ringing, Cook's voiceover explained, 'A few days earlier, Harry started recording his phone calls. No-one knows why'. The edited recording was then played, with Cook noting that 'This is the only caller that police have not been able to identify' and that 'To agree to an early morning meeting was very unlike' Harry, who was 'a late riser'. Following further interviews and appeals for other information,

Flash Harry

the sequence concluded with a different edit of the recording that featured just the caller's voice, including some new phrases — 'too early for you?', 'perfect, perfect', 'he's gone away, he's left them with his missus', 'down there, won't be long, about ten or 15 minutes' and 'down the other side of Robertsbridge'.

In an interview with the lead detective after the reconstruction, Cook observed that the meeting time arranged at the call's end meant that the caller 'has got to be your prime suspect'. Detective Superintendent Graham Hill would only say that 'there may be some reason' why the caller hasn't come forward to date, asking anyone who recognised him — or the caller himself 'if he wants to be eliminated' — to get in touch. At the end of the show, Cook reported that the show's call centre had received 60 calls about a different murder (the still unsolved killing of businesswoman Jean Bradley in West London a fortnight earlier) as well as robberies, an abduction and a rape, but nothing about the Fuller case. However, Sheila Hall, watching *Crimewatch* that night, instantly recognised the caller as her brother-in-law, as did his neighbour. When she raised the show with him the next day, he denied being the caller. But he went to the police two days after the broadcast, carrying a typed letter stating that he had called Harry the evening before his death.

This chain of events demonstrates how useful *Crimewatch* can be to the police. However, the programme's precise role in the investigation of Harry's death is less clear. The police had already spoken to Hall's brother-in-law in their initial sweep of the car dealer's acquaintances well before the broadcast. At that time, he told them that he had last spoken to the car dealer by phone five days before he died. It seems that police — who waited two weeks for a forensic team to painstakingly analyse Blackmans Cottage before they conducted a search for potentially relevant documents — had not discovered the recorded message by then. The tape, containing 49 minutes of recorded phone conversations, was in a Geemarc answering machine under a sofa. Once it was found, the police must have quickly revisited their list of Harry's acquaintances, because the tape contained an important clue about the caller's identity.

Apparently referring to an unpublished part of the call, Cook concluded her interview by asking the detective 'Do you think [the caller] might be called Steve?' and received the answer: 'There was an indication that he might'. Clearly, the police would have taken a very close look at (and listened especially carefully to the voice of) anyone named Steve who was linked to Harry. Perhaps there were many Steves in Harry's circle and the police were unable to narrow down the caller to a particular one. Or maybe they could and were already focussing on Stephen Young, Hall's brother-in-law and Harry's insurance broker. Nevertheless, playing the tape on the BBC plausibly served several investigative purposes. It could generate independent evidence of the caller's identity by prompting those who knew him to come forward. And it could also prompt the caller himself to come forward. One week after the *Crimewatch* broadcast, the police announced Young's arrest for Harry's murder.

Pillar of the community

> Ray said, 'How?' The glass spelt 'shot'. Ray said something else and the glass spelt 'shotgun and pistol.' Ray said, 'Where is the gun?' The glass spelt 'Police'.

It is not easy to explore a complex event via a séance. The makeshift Ouija board's response to Ray's 'How?' was a mixture of the obvious and the unlikely. There was never any doubt that Harry died because he was shot and, as revealed by the post-mortem, that the fatal bullet came from a small-calibre weapon fired at close range. On the other hand, the police insisted that they never found the murder weapon. Perhaps what Ray really wanted to know was how an insurance broker with no criminal record could shoot anyone in the back, especially with a 'dum-dum' bullet that had been 'filed' to cause 'maximum damage'.

Stephen Young is Harry Fuller's opposite in nearly every respect. While Harry was onto his third marriage at age 45, Young, a decade younger, had been married to his 'attractive wife, Sally' for 12 years. The couple lived in Pembury, where Young had grown up, ten miles to the north of Wadhurst over the county border, with their two boys then aged eleven and nine. The family owned their semi-detached house, inherited from Young's father. The insurance broker

> was a popular member of the Pembury Football Club, helping to run the under-11s team. He made donations to the club and once bought a new strip for the junior team out of his own pocket.

Young's eldest captained the team that year, when they narrowly lost the Crowborough Cup to nearby Paddock Wood. A member of a Masonic lodge, a star performer in the village pantomime and the treasurer for the 21st Kent Home Guard Rifle Club, Young was 'a pillar of the community'.

As the head of the police investigation readily acknowledged after the trial:

> Outwardly Stephen Young was a very responsible family man who was well liked by his clients and people in Pembury. But there was a totally different side to him and it was that other side that very few people knew about.

The most prominent symbol of Young's 'other side' was a photo that featured repeatedly in newspaper accounts of the case. At a desk sits a police officer, Detective Inspector Stuart Booth, holding parts of a long-barrelled rifle. A piece of military artillery and half a dozen bundles of bullets rest beside his elbow. To Booth's right are a collection of telescopic sights, to his left a small handgun. On each side are open suitcases containing an array of weapons, parts and ammunition, with disguises—a black balaclava and a hairy wig—laid across the top. The foreground is dominated by a bizarre rubber mask, resembling an orc from the *Lord of the Rings* movies.

According to the police, Young

> kept a secret arsenal which included sawn-off shotguns, de-activated grenade launchers, imitation sub-machine guns, bayonets, and thousands of rounds of ammunition. Police also found a collection of combat gear, wigs,

masks and false car number plates. Mr Hill said: 'There was enough to fill a medium-sized room. They were scattered all over the place'.

Another account said that the police's 'raid' yielded enough weapons to 'fill a squash court', including 'a fake rocket-launcher, a Rambo-style grenade-launcher and a loaded pistol under his young son's bed' — the latter was a 9 mm 'Browning pistol which had been modified in a way which did not suggest that it had any legitimate purpose'. An anonymous detective provocatively described Young as 'a Michael Ryan waiting to happen', a reference to a 27-year-old with an obsession for firearms who amassed a lawful arsenal before using it to kill 16 people and himself in Hungerford, Berkshire in 1987. That incident prompted legislative bans in England on semi-automatic weapons and various shotguns.

However, the police's search warrant did not uncover a gun of the type they believed had been used to kill Harry — a .32 calibre weapon. They did find a total of 61 rounds of .32 bullets at Young's home and his Pembury high street office, as well as a 'reloading machine' that could be used to make bullets out of recycled ammunition. At Young's trial, the Home Office firearm's expert, Malcolm Fletcher, testified that 'excess pressure' had been used to reload the bullets found at Blackmans Cottage and that grooves on those bullets were similar to those on Young's recycling machine. As well, Fletcher testified that marks on a fired bullet found in Young's home matched the ones in Wadhurst:

> Both cartridges from the murder scene, as well as a dummy bullet found at Young's home had been fired from the same gun and I have absolutely no doubt of this.

Some of the bullets at Young's home had been altered into dum-dum rounds of the sort that were used to kill Harry. While Young held licences for two Smith and Wesson handguns, a 9 mm pistol and a rifle, he initially told the police that he did not own any .32 ammunition or a .32 weapon.

According to one juror's affidavit, the Ouija board at one point mentioned a 'Walther PPK' — famous as James Bond's weapon of choice—but this was no mystical revelation or even guesswork. At the trial, Young admitted that he had bought a Chinese-made replica .32 Walther PPK by mail order in 1988. A later police investigation of gun-trafficking in Britain from 1994 to 2000 revealed that Young had purchased it from Regional Instauration Firearms Little Eaton (RIFLE), an antique gun shop belonging to a father and son, William and Mitchell Greenwood. The Greenwoods lost their licence to deal in firearms in 1994 after being found in possession of a weapon prohibited after the Hungerford massacre, but they continued to sell firearms deactivated by the Home Office, supposedly for collectors or as decorations. The police said that the Greenwoods were well aware that some buyers intended to reactivate the weapons, often with instructions or parts supplied by the father and son. A decade after Harry's death, one of the detectives told the media:

> From inquiries resulting from this investigation, we have also secured the arrests of 40 other people and recovered a total of 420 firearms. The Greenwoods stuck two fingers up at the law and were looking for a loophole to try to supply firearms. The reactivation of weapons has been one of the main sources of firearms to criminals in this country and in my view deactivated firearms should be banned altogether, or more stringently licensed. From a very quiet backwater, their firearms have turned up on the streets of Manchester and London. This is a key turning point in the fight against guns, as they were, in effect, the quartermasters to the criminal underworld.

The Greenwoods admitted the sales but denied all responsibility for their customers' actions, including Young's. In 2004, aged 76 and 42, they were each convicted of conspiracy and sentenced to seven years' imprisonment.

English rose

> Ray also asked who killed Nicola, and the glass spelt out 'Stephen Young'.

On the same day Stephen Young was remanded in custody before a Lewes magistrate, a procession of over 50 cars travelled five miles from Dunorlan Park in Tunbridge Wells, past Pembury and onto the historic village of Matfield. The police provided 'special traffic control' to help the cortège through town to St Luke's Church. At the procession's head was a 'heavily decorated' hearse bearing Harry Fuller's coffin and a vintage Rolls Royce carrying his immediate family (The funeral notice described Harry as the 'Beloved Son of Mr and Mrs C Fuller and a very dear Brother'). After a 'standing room only' service, Harry was buried in the churchyard, next to the graves of his recently deceased aunt Phoebe (and later his uncle Fred, who died 13 years to the day after Harry) and his grandparents John and Amy. The church's Reverend Robert Middlewick observed that 'any death was sad but that death in violent circumstances was particularly sad' and 'against God's ordinance'.

The next day 'in a more low-key ceremony' attended by senior detectives investigating the case, Nicola Fuller's death was mourned in St Mark's Church in Tunbridge Wells, 'the same church where her marriage to Harry was blessed just eight months ago' after the couple's wedding at Tunbridge Wells Register Office. Reverend Francis Cumberledge, who had performed the blessing, said of Nicola's death:

> You cannot make sense of a nonsense like this. Someone deliberately killing someone else makes no sense whatsoever—we have got to stand together in our common grief and sadness of it all.

His sermon urged the congregation, including Nicola's parents and her sister, 'to look to God who suffered for them on the cross'. Afterwards, three cars accompanied Nicola's body to the Kent and Sussex Crematorium.

The shooting of a man in his 40s, possibly by an acquaintance in his 30s, while shocking, falls short of being a national tragedy. Rather, it was Nicola's simultaneous death that gave the event its notoriety in Wadhurst and beyond, well before the jurors used their makeshift Ouija board. Nicola's parents, Michael and Barbara Johnson, both aged 51, took on the public role of the crime's living victims. In a press conference a week after the couple's death, Michael called for public assistance as Barbara sobbed beside him:

> Our beloved daughter was brutally murdered. She was an innocent witness. Both families are totally devastated. Please come forward and trust the police. I can see no reason why there should be anything to fear.

Tragically, it was Nicola's parents who had first raised the alarm. Barbara told *Crimewatch*:

> Nicky had gone to a reunion on Tuesday night and I hadn't spoken or seen her since Sunday, so I decided to ring her at 8:45 and I rang and the line was engaged and I continued to ring every five minutes until quarter past nine.

Decades later, she recalled precisely what came next:

> When I rang her work and she had not been in, I rang Michael and said something was wrong. We got to Wadhurst and her car was in the car park. We could see her keys and bag were on the table at the back door. Between the lounge and the kitchen, there was a utility room and there was Harry's feet sticking out from the door.

Their worst fears were realised when the police broke into the cottage that evening. Michael recalled: 'A police officer had gone upstairs and called me up. There was Nicky'. His wife added: 'It was like watching a film, only I was involved in it. It must have been awful for Michael having to go and identify her.'

Nicola was found in the couple's bedroom wearing a dressing gown, with a duvet over her face and a pool of her blood beside a phone handset.

A trail of blood led to a landing, where a coffee cup and cigarette had fallen. The two bodies were removed in turn the next morning and transported to the Eastbourne District General Hospital on the Channel shore. The autopsy was carried out by Iain West, feted on his death seven years later as 'the foremost forensic pathologist in Britain', whose cases included the shooting of policewoman Yvonne Fletcher by (what West determined was) a single bullet fired from the Libyan embassy. West found that Nicola had been shot in the shoulder from behind, in the forehead after she turned to face the shooter and again 'through her left cheek'. A final bullet fired through the duvet ended her life. Barbara told *Crimewatch*: 'She seems to have found happiness and suddenly had it snatched away from her. It's so dreadful that anyone could do that to her'.

Many characterised the couple as an oddity. Next door's tea room proprietor described Harry as 'a thick set man and his wife … a slim woman with light brown long hair'. As one newspaper summed-up, 'He was a dodgy car dealer, she was a lovely girl'. Young's prosecutor would later tell his jury:

> He dealt in cash and often had a wad of notes on him or even a briefcase full of money. He had people who would shun him and people who disliked him intensely. Nicola was a different person altogether—younger, quieter and more sensitive.

Nicola's grieving father said that his daughter:

> …was an English Rose, very unassuming and very quiet. She would never do anything to hurt someone if she could do something to please or help them. She would have been totally devastated by all of this. She was totally innocent. She knew nothing of her husband's business dealings.

Her mother told *Crimewatch* that she was a 'private, dainty little girl, really'. The *Sussex Courier* published a photo of Nicola taken a week before her death as she was working the free gift-wrapping table at Royal Victoria Place shopping centre in Tunbridge Wells. The photographer explained that she 'refused to give her name', describing her as 'very shy'.

Nicola met Harry because of the marriage of her younger sister, Michelle, to a friend of Harry's. When Michelle introduced the pair in June of 1992, Harry 'asked Nicola to ferry some auction cars for him'. The couple married in August, while living in a flat in Broadwater Lane, Tunbridge Wells, before their move to Wadhurst. At the press conference, Michael said that the 27-year-old had been 'looking for someone special' the previous summer and Harry 'fit[ted] the bill'. He added:

> I was unhappy they were getting married so quickly, I thought they should wait and get to know each other a little more. Nicola was strong-willed and insisted on going ahead with the wedding straightaway.

He told *Crimewatch* that 'It was like a roller-coaster once it started and there was no way of stopping it'.

Despite their belief that Harry's business dealings had brought a killer to their daughter's home, there was no hint of anger from Nicola's family directed to the family's newest member. To the contrary, 'Nicola was happier than I had seen her for months' and Harry 'seemed to bring Nicky out of her shell and she seemed to really enjoy life being with him'. Harry 'was always protective of Nicky and there was always a house full of flowers'. He 'was always the perfect son-in-law' and 'a very likable character, though he seemed to come from a different way of life than we were used to'. Reverend Cumberledge said he had met the pair:

> …a couple of times to discuss the service and I got the impression that Mr Fuller saw this as a chance for a new start in life. He said to me that money wasn't everything and he hoped to start afresh with Nicola. She was a very quiet person.

Nicola's father added:

> They were very happy. We grew to like him very much. They used to come here for Sunday lunch most weekends. He seemed to be looking for a family unit and he certainly became a very popular member of the family.

The *Crimewatch* reconstruction showed Nicola preparing to attend a reunion with school friends as Harry received his phone call for a meeting the next morning, and him picking her up from an Italian restaurant in Tunbridge Wells at 11 pm. A friend of Nicola's said that the couple were 'very happy' and had booked a Canary Islands holiday for the following week.

The recent marriage gave the national media their angle. *The Sun* placed the couple's wedding photo — Harry with a wide grin and loud boutonniere, his wife with flowers in her hair as the couple cut the cake — on its front page, with the accompanying headline, 'Mum-to-be and her new husband are shot dead in their cottage'. The article's lead was the revelation, attributed to 'police', that Nicola, 'a bride of six months … was pregnant' when she died. The story quoted 'a friend in the village':

> I heard that Harry had some shady deals. But whatever he did, it's tragic that a poor young wife looking forward to motherhood should have to die too. Nicola hadn't told everyone about the baby but was privately thrilled about it and looking forward to the birth.

Today claimed that Nicola 'was expecting their first child within weeks', implicitly explaining the couples' speedy wedding half a year before.

But a few days later Detective Chief Inspector Alan Snelling 'emphatically denied newspaper reports that the murdered woman was pregnant'. Meanwhile, the photographer who took the couple's wedding photo revealed that he received an anonymous warning the day after the couple's deaths that 'if you give out the pictures you are dead meat'. At the press conference, Michael said that Nicola 'would have been very unhappy with the release of her picture to the national press without her family's permission.' The media promptly dropped the motherhood angle, settled into describing the couple as 'newlyweds' but continued to prominently feature their wedding photos. In August 1993, a magistrate committed Young for trial, having first cleared the court at the police's request, citing the 'grounds of public order, security and safety', and then refusing a renewed application for bail.

Rolls of cash

> Previously Ray had asked the motive and the glass spelt out 'money'. Ray asked where it was and the glass spelt 'case'. He then asked how much had been taken and the glass spelt out '63,000'. Ray asked where the money was now and the glass spelt out 'bag'. Ray asked where and the glass spelt out 'Harry Brinklow, room above office'.

Within days of the deaths, *Today* reported:

> Police believe the killer of 'Flash' Harry Fuller and his wife Nicola could be the third person in a love triangle. Detectives have been interviewing former wives and girlfriends of Fuller, 45, found on Wednesday shot through the heart at his cottage in Wadhurst, Sussex. They think it significant that Nicola, 27, was shot in the head.

Doubtless, the investigating police would later have wondered whether it was mere coincidence that Nicola Fuller and Stephen Young both came from the same small town.

Pembury was the same size as Wadhurst, but its character was dominated by being just outside a town of 100,000. A local councillor commenting in the *Pembury Village News* in 1993 painted a grim picture:

> The majority of Pembury people if asked where they live would reply in a village. But do they? The post war town styled estates have created, dare I write, a suburb of Tunbridge Wells. These developments in relation to the existing village broke up the community. The newcomers were mainly young, from urban areas wishing to create a new and better world; the older villagers, perhaps resenting the sudden change were slow to accept. The village growth was too fast, the schools, shops, roads and amenity facilities were more than over stretched, the local industries disappeared or reduced in size resulting in a population of commuters.

Nicola (until she married) and Young both lived in Pembury's eastern side, with the Youngs' Heskett Park house only half a mile from the Johnsons' in The Gill. But Young's prosecutors presented no evidence of any link between Young and Nicola, other than Harry.

At Young's trial, the prosecution emphasised Harry's penchant for carrying cash. In his opening argument, prosecutor Michael Lawson said that Harry had recently received £13,000 from a neighbour as capital to buy second-hand cars, with the profit to be split 50-50. However, the police never found that money in Blackmans Cottage, instead locating only a total of £210 distributed between a shoe in a wardrobe and under the couple's sofa. The prosecution said that Young knew of the loan from the neighbour and would have been aware of Harry's hoarding of cash via his insurance brokerage. Indeed, the *Argus* reported a colourful account of Young's first meeting with Harry ten years earlier:

> Harry Fuller swaggered into his insurance broker's office, opened a briefcase crammed with banknotes and asked a young clerk to count the cash. The wide-eyed office worker counted the money three times before reaching a total of more than £23,000. Harry thanked him, snapped the case shut and left without a word of explanation.

Even Nicola's father had a tale about a briefcase full of banknotes:

> He asked me to hide the case behind the settee in my living room while we went out for a restaurant meal. I knew that he kept briefcases full of money at Blackmans Cottage. He said it was from car sales but, I must say, I wasn't convinced. I was glad to see him collect it.

He added that Harry had no wallet, instead preferring to carry 'rolls of cash' in his pockets.

The prosecution also had evidence that Young desperately needed money. His insurance brokerage, Young and Harding Associates, had not made a profit in the past eight years and he was unable to service its debts. The family's inherited house had several mortgages with payments in arrears. According to Lawson:

At the end of 1992 he was being threatened with legal action from the building society and the bank had been constantly at him to reduce his overdraft.

By the time of the Fullers' deaths, Young's debts totalled more than £100,000. He had borrowed money from others, including £20,000 from his wife's family and £6,500 from a close friend, Harry Brinklow, who was namechecked in the jurors' séance.

At the trial, the prosecution presented further circumstantial evidence in the form of the Provincial Insurance Company, which had demanded that Young pay £13,500 by 10th February 1993, the same day the Fullers died. The company's representative, Martin Bell, testified that Young met him that morning and handed over a post-dated cheque for £6,000. The cheque cleared the next day despite Young's overdraft, because the broker had just deposited the required amount into his bank account in £20 notes. He also paid off an overdue phone bill for £360. Dismissing the possibility that much more cash had been stolen—a scenario seemingly pressed by the jurors' makeshift Ouija board—the prosecution's theory was that Young's crimes at Blackmans Cottage failed to resolve his financial problems. The broker spent the days after the murders writing letters to friends and acquaintances pleading for further loans.

Inner circle

> We then discussed among ourselves what we should do and the glass spelt out 'Tell police'. I said 'We can't'. It then spelt out 'later, us and you'. It continued, 'Vote guilty tomorrow'.

Before asking about the money, Ray 'cut up paper and put numbers from 0 to 10 on them and put them in an inner circle. The alphabet was on an outer circle.' But the jurors' makeshift Ouija board still differed in a key way from commercial ones, which feature the word 'Goodbye', allowing the séance to unambiguously end. Instead, it was up to the jurors themselves to call it a night:

> During this time Ray made notes. It is only right to say I was crying by this time and the other ladies were upset as well. We realised it had gone too far and we ended the exercise. Ray threw the paper away.

There is plenty more left to be said about Young, Harry and (most tragically of all) Nicola. But Ray's mini-jury didn't ask any more that night and the Court of Appeal's summary didn't dig any further:

> On 10 February 1993, the dead bodies of Harry Fuller and Nicola Fuller were found at their cottage home in East Sussex. They had both been shot. The appellant ran an insurance business in Sussex and was authorised to hold firearms. A recorded message on the deceased's answerphone indicated that the appellant was due to meet Harry Fuller at the cottage on 10 February. The Crown's case was that Harry Fuller, a second-hand car dealer known to deal in cash, had conducted a cash transaction the day before his death and the appellant, being short of cash, had gone to the cottage on 10 February, had killed Harry Fuller for his money and shot Nicola to silence her. The next day, the appellant paid cash into a bank account and was able to settle a debt. Reliance was placed upon bullets and cartridge cases recovered from the deceased's cottage which were of the same make, type and size as ammunition recovered from the appellant's home and bore markings which showed that all had been fired from the same gun.

The next stage of the Ouija board case is told in the Court of Appeal's judgement.

CHAPTER 3

Only a Game

The talking board — The most bizarre appeal — Beyond the evidence — An awkward decision — The heart of the case — The greatest Lord Chief Justice

Nearly two decades before Stephen Young's appeal, at lunchtime on Sunday 5th October 1975, eleven-year-old Lesley Molseed went missing on a brief errand. Her body was found three days later on a steep hillside with knife wounds on her shoulders and semen stains on her underwear. The police investigation eventually focused on a local tax clerk, 22-year-old Stefan Kiszko, who combined the clichéd stereotype of a sex offender (a strange appearance, sexual immaturity and no friends other than his mother) with mild circumstantial evidence of guilt (false alibis, claims of indecent exposure, recent testosterone treatments and a piece of paper recording a licence plate number that matched a car that often drove past Molseed's resting place). He confessed to the police and was convicted the following year by a 10-2 majority jury verdict, one of several high-profile victories that decade by his prosecutor, Peter Taylor QC. Such successes vindicated Taylor's 1950 decision to choose a life in the law over one as a promising pianist.

Taylor, appointed as a judge in 1980, likewise owed his rise to the top of England's judicial hierarchy to 1970s prosecutions. In the early 1990s, the reputation of British criminal justice was savaged by a series of cases — the Birmingham Six, the Guildford Four, the Maguire Seven, the Tottenham Three — where decades-old murder or terrorism convictions were belatedly overturned. These cases carried hard lessons not just for forensic scientists, police and prosecutors, but judges too. The highest profile of the latter was England's Lord Chief Justice during the 1980s, Geoffrey Lane, who had dismissed the Birmingham Six's appeal in 1988, saying 'the verdict of the jury was correct'. After those same convictions were overturned by his court just three years later, newspaper editorials and parliamentary motions demanded his resignation and the government established a Royal Commission into the criminal justice system. Lane held on for another year, allowing him to correct a further stain on English criminal justice.

In the intervening 17 years, Kiszko's mother Charlotte waged a largely lone campaign to have her son's murder conviction revisited. It reached its fruition in 1990 when solicitors presented a case for executive clemency, based on fresh evidence supporting the tax clerk's alibi and doubting the allegations of indecent exposure. Coincidentally, the application was settled on the day that Kiszko's trial lawyer, David Waddington QC, was appointed as Home Secretary, nominally (at that time) in charge of investigating fresh evidence. The ensuing police inquiry uncovered previously undisclosed evidence of sperm in the semen on Molseed's clothes, ruling out the sexually immature Kiszko as the source. On 18th February 1992, the Court of Appeal, with Lord Lane presiding, quashed Kiszko's conviction. A week later, Lane announced his resignation. In another coincidence, his successor as Lord Chief Justice was Kiszko's prosecutor.

On his appointment as head of England's courts, Taylor distinguished himself by engaging directly with the public. He held an unprecedented press conference and promised further ones at six-monthly intervals. He also became the first sitting judge to appear on a prominent political discussion show, the BBC's *Question Time*. Reflecting his view that his predecessor was unfairly maligned, he later explained:

> If judges do speak out on topics which concern the public they may overcome the widely held belief, stemming from all those years of lofty reticence, that they are out of touch or even, as has been said, living on another planet. It should not be done too often, but it can and does have a role to play in the evolution and development of a sound legal system in which the public can have confidence.

His appointment as England's top judge gave him a further platform: a seat in the House of Lords. In his inaugural speech on a bill to alter the judicial retirement age, Baron Taylor of Gosforth said:

> Apart from the trepidation natural to a maiden speaker addressing this illustrious House I have today two additional embarrassments. First, as I have only recently taken office, it may seem premature and indeed perhaps defeatist for me to be speaking of retirement…

His second 'embarrassment', that he would stray into 'controversy' when addressing the merits of the proposed legislation, became a cherished hallmark of his time as Lord Chief Justice. Doubtless, Taylor would have been truly embarrassed to know that, just 30 months later, he would be writing a judgement about Ouija boards. And no-one would have foreseen that, by then, his brilliant career would be nearly over.

The Court of Appeal's reasons for their judgement in *R v Young* marked the moment when the Ouija board case switched from tabloid fodder to the official record. After addressing the law on juror secrecy (discussed in *Chapter Five*), the balance of the court's reasons dealt with an unprecedented question: whether a criminal defendant must receive a new trial if some of his jurors used a Ouija board. As this chapter explains, this question is by no means straightforward and the Court of Appeal's brief answer raises still more questions.

The talking board

> The word 'Ouija' is simply a combination of the French word 'oui' and the German word 'ja' and means therefore 'yes, yes'. An ouija board is used at a séance to seek messages from the spirits of absent or deceased persons.

The Court of Appeal's account of the word 'Ouija', while supported in some dictionaries, is the least appealing of several such explanations. After all, why would an American invention that in its standard form prominently features the English words 'Yes' and 'No' be named after an amalgamation of (mispronounced) foreign equivalents of just one of those words, 'Oui' and 'Ja'? A more satisfactory alternative account is the following from the 1890s:

> Charles Kennard stated that he named the new board Ouija (pronounced wE-ja) after a session with Miss Peters, Elijah Bond's sister-in-law: 'I remarked that we had not yet settled upon a name, and as the board had helped us in other ways, we would ask it to propose one. It spelled out O-U-I-J-A. When I asked the meaning of the word it said 'Good Luck'. Miss Peters there upon drew upon her neck a chain which had at the end a locket, on it a figure of a woman and at the top the word 'Ouija'. We asked her if she had thought of the name, and she said she had not. We then adopted the word.'

The woman in the locket may well have been English novelist and activist Maria Louise Ramé, widely known as Ouida (her pen-name, a childhood mispronunciation of her middle name). At the start of the 20th-century, there were dozens of different names attached to similar boards. Much like new media start-ups today, Ouija emerged supreme through a combination of catchiness, luck and canny marketing by the trademark's various owners.

The history of Ouija boards, a topic entirely neglected in the Court of Appeal's judgement, commences with the growth of spiritualism amongst middle-class and upper-class Americans in the mid-19th-century, in part as a response to civil war casualties. Doubts about paid mediums led to a preference for techniques that did not require a third-party interlocutor. The initially favoured methods were table-turning, where participants held a table that moved when letters of the alphabet were called out, and automatic writing, where participants touched a 'planchette' (a tiny moveable wooden board) attached to a pen. Both methods are readily explicable as instances of the ideomotor effect, where participants' unconscious muscular movements (or, for the more sceptical, a fraudulent participant's deliberate motions) translate into meaningful responses that seem to be (and, for the less sceptical, are) the result of an external force.

But the two early methods were respectively laborious and illegible, and were supplanted when a combined approach became wildly popular. In 1886, the *New York Daily Tribune* reported:

'Planchette is simply nowhere,' said a Western man at the Fifth Avenue Hotel, 'compared with the new scheme for mysterious communication that is being used out in Ohio. I know of whole communities that are wild over the "talking board," as some of them call it. I have never heard any name for it. But I have seen and heard some of the most remarkable things about its operations—things that seem to pass all human comprehension or explanation.

What is the board like?

Give me a pencil and I will show you. The first requisite is the operating board. It may be rectangular, about 18 x 20 inches. It is inscribed like this: The 'yes' and the 'no' are to start and stop the conversation. The 'good-evening' and 'good-night' are for courtesy. Now a little table three or four inches high is prepared with four legs. Any one can make the whole apparatus in fifteen minutes with a jack-knife and a marking brush. You take the board in your lap, another person sitting down with you. You each grasp the little table with the thumb and forefinger at each corner next to you. Then the question is asked, 'Are there any communications?' Pretty soon you think the other person is pushing the table. He thinks you are doing the same. But the table moves around to 'yes' or 'no'. Then you go on asking questions and the answers are spelled out by the legs of the table resting on the letters one after the other.'

Despite (or perhaps because of) the easy manufacture of such devices, entrepreneurs soon seized on the idea, including lawyer Elijah Bond and the various other founders of Baltimore's Kennard Novelty Company, who trademarked and patented their Ouija board in 1890. When members of the group fell out or lost interest, the rights were left in the hands of a company employee, William Fuld, who aggressively developed and defended the company's intellectual property during a renewed talking board craze on university campuses after World War One.

The popular appeal of Ouija boards is partly explained by Fuld's clever marketing, which pitched them at believers and non-believers alike:

> Ouija knows all the answers. Weird and mysterious. Surpasses, in its unique results, mind reading, clairvoyance and second sight. It furnishes never failing amusement and recreation for the entire family. As unexplainable as Hindu magic—more intense and absorbingly interesting than a mystery story. Ouija gives you entertainment you have never experienced. It draws the two people using it into close companionship and weaves about them a feeling of mysterious isolation. Unquestionably the most fascinating entertainment for modern people and modern life.

Such marketing prompted a legal dispute in the early-1920s about whether Ouija boards were subject to a ten per cent tax aimed at various luxury goods, including 'chess and checker boards and pieces, dice, games and parts of games (except playing cards and children's toys and games)'. After a federal judge held that the tax applied to talking boards (ruling that the boards resemble 'games of solitaire' and that, while 'childish', the boards would not interest many children), one appeal judge responded that:

> ...the Ouija board has no real likeness in construction or use to any of the specified articles. It is unique, in a class by itself, plainly different and distinguishable from any of the enumerated games. If not strictly sui generis, it is more like the physical appliances used by those who pretend to predict the future...[I]n view of the peculiar character of the Ouija board and the serious use to which it is put by thousands of persons, it is by no means certain, if indeed it be probable, that the Congress would have included it by express mention if the matter had been brought to its attention.

However, a majority of the federal circuit court upheld the original ruling:

> It seems safe to say psychologists recognize the Ouija board as a real means of expression of automotism. The court knows in a general way that the Ouija board is seriously used by some persons in the belief that it affords mysterious spirit communication; by others as a means of personal observation of the control of muscular or nervous action by the subconscious or unconscious mind. But the court cannot pretend to be ignorant that it is very largely sold with the expectation that it is to be used merely as a means of social amusement or play, and is actually so used. It is true that automotism is the basis of this use, but phenomena of psychical as well as of physical nature may be the basis of amusement and games.

The United States Supreme Court refused a further appeal, but 15 years later ruled that the circuit court went too far in allowing the taxing of 'all instrumentalities, not necessary for comfort, whose chief use is to afford amusement and diversion ... Knitting for diversion is not a "game"; nor is horseback riding.' Ruling that a jigsaw puzzle fell outside the statute, the Supreme Court observed that 'The ouija board is wholly different from the puzzle here under consideration'. Regardless, Fuld's children (after his suitably bizarre death in 1927 from accidentally falling from one of his buildings) continued to market the boards as a form of family entertainment. The boards experienced further waves of popularity as a 'parlour game', even outselling Monopoly during the 1960s.

The Court of Appeal's account never mentions that the 1994 owner of the trademark 'Ouija' was a familiar name, Parker Brothers, best known for Monopoly, Cluedo, Risk and Trivial Pursuit. Later purchased by Hasbro, it marketed various versions of Ouija boards with the tagline 'It's only a game, isn't it?' By the 1990s, however, Ouija boards had lost popularity, following decades of decline in interest in both spiritualism and parlour games. The ideomotor effect that underlay the boards' operation is now seen as more fraud than fun, especially after its repeated exposure as a means for deceit and abuse in the context of so-called 'facilitated-communication' with the severely disabled. The result is that sceptics and believers alike deprecate using the boards as entertainment, with each warning that they could be a vehicle for victimisation by wrongdoers, respectively terrestrial and astral. These developments have been duly tracked in the popular sphere by the appearance of Ouija boards in supernatural movies, including in a pivotal scene of the 1972 film *The Exorcist* and as the central plot device in the later *Witchboard* trilogy (whose middle movie had its European release in the same year as Young's trial and appeal).

Before setting out the unnamed juror's account of the hotel room events, the Court of Appeal (presumably relying on one or more other affidavits) described the initial reaction to this topic of conversation in the following terms:

> After dinner, there was conversation amongst some of the jurors about ouija boards. One of the bailiffs spoke out strongly against them as did a lady juror, and the other bailiff agreed, saying 'not to be so stupid'.

The bailiffs' and lone juror's view was most likely the majority one in 1994, albeit generally held in ignorance of the device's earlier history, prevalence and marketing. Today, fans of Ouija boards (and, perhaps, shareholders of Hasbro) optimistically predict their contemporary revival, sparked by new entertainment franchises (such as the 2016 and 2014, and 2007, and 2003, *Ouija* movies) and their celebration in parts of the internet. This decade, Hasbro experimented with glow-in-the-dark Ouija boards and an all-pink model seemingly aimed at teenage (tween) girls, while others sell Ouija board underwear. More ominously for judges, smartphone users can now readily download Ouija board apps that respond to both voice and touch, combining past and present anxieties about juror misconduct.

The most bizarre appeal

> In our view, what occurred in the present case was not merely objectionable but amounted to a material irregularity.

At a late stage of Stefan Kiszko's trial for the murder of Lesley Molseed, a juror revealed that she had overheard a prosecutor in a pub saying that Kiszko's counsel had advised him to plead guilty. The trial judge, after asking the trial's two barristers—(future Lord Chief Justice) Peter Taylor QC and (future Home Secretary) David Waddington QC—for their views, ruled that the juror could remain on the panel and the trial could go on. A year later, the Court of Appeal held that there was no miscarriage of justice:

> No doubt his view was based on the almost self-evident proposition that in these circumstances any intelligent juror would have realised that the advice [Kiszko] had been given by his counsel was to plead guilty to manslaughter on the ground of diminished responsibility.

Lord Bridge added that there was 'nothing in' Waddington's admitted failure to seek instructions from Kiszko himself about the matter.

Fifteen years later, the Royal Commission on Criminal Justice declared that the Court of Appeal 'is crucial to the early detection of miscarriages of justice' and recommended that it be more willing to hear new evidence and overturn jury findings. A year ahead of Stephen Young's appeal, it concluded:

> We do not think the Court of Appeal is well constituted to supervise and direct police or other investigations. Nor do we think the same body should exercise investigative as well as judicial functions.

Rather, it recommended that the post-conviction investigative role be given to its proposed new Criminal Cases Review Commission. In addition to reviewing cases on its own, the Royal Commission recommended that the new body could also supervise investigations on behalf of the Court of Appeal, the same role that the Treasury Solicitor would play in Young's appeal.

The other change the Royal Commission recommended for English appeals was to replace the statutory provision that governed when jury convictions could be overturned. Since 1966, the Court of Appeal could quash convictions if it 'thought' that:

> (a) the verdict of the jury should be set aside on the ground that under all the circumstances of the case it is unsafe or unsatisfactory; or
>
> (b) the judgement of the court of trial should be set aside on the ground of a wrong decision on any question of law; or
>
> (c) there was a material irregularity in the course of the trial.

The problem, everyone agreed, is that this provision was itself unsatisfactory, especially as the first ground seemed to subsume the rest. A majority of the Royal Commission favoured a new simple, single appeal ground that a conviction is 'unsafe', an idea the minority disliked because:

> ...this expression implies that there is something wrong with the jury's verdict, whether it was unsupported by the evidence or affected by some irregularity or error. There might, however, be some irregularities or errors of law or procedure which did not necessarily affect the jury's verdict but were so serious that the conviction could not stand.

This description perfectly captures the dilemma the Court of Appeal would face in Young's appeal. Nevertheless, the majority view prevailed in Parliament, with the strong support of Baron Taylor in the House of Lords.

Young's appeal, which came too early for this legislative change, showcased the problems of the old appeal provision. The appeal was fought over the question of whether or not there was a 'material irregularity' at the trial, rather than whether the jury reached the right verdict. Decades of applying the confusing 1966 provision left the Court of Appeal with no clear test to apply to the unique situation before it. The one example that counsel could point to was the position taken by the Court of Appeal a year earlier in dismissing the challenge (discussed in *Chapter One*) based on a businessman's use of a mobile phone in the jury room. There, the court had said:

> This call was an outgoing call, it was made by a man who had expressed concern as to the state of his business and there is no reason for disbelieving him when he says it related solely to his business and was a very short call concerned simply with whether there had been an expected delivery. In those circumstances we are clearly of the view that there was no material irregularity in this case.

This leaves unresolved the question of whether an outgoing call that does concern the case at hand is always a material irregularity and whether that remains true even when the 'call' is placed by (makeshift) Ouija board. The three judges who heard Young's appeal had no useful precedents to guide them.

Taylor repeatedly acted to ensure that he, and the two judges who initially sat with him, would be the final decision-makers in Young's appeal. At the end of the matter's first hearing in June, he said 'We would wish if possible to hear it in the present constitution'—that, is, the same three judges—'since we have looked at the papers'. At that point, the 'papers' consisted solely of Adrian's three-page letter, plus a covering letter from a solicitor and reports from two bailiffs. A fortnight later, Taylor again said:

> As to a hearing, we would propose that this matter should be brought back to the court in the present constitution, if that is possible, and if it is to be the present constitution, I think it would have to be some stage in mid-July. We will try and find a date.

By then, there had been a morning of arguments and an afternoon of procedural discussions, but there were no additional papers to read.

The Ouija Board Jurors

Despite the possibility of jurors' being called as witnesses, the Lord Chief Justice nevertheless pressed for a July hearing when many Britons are on holiday, but the next hearing scotched that plan. The parties needed time to read the 15 affidavits the Treasury Solicitor had obtained. Labelling the situation 'unfortunate', Taylor advised the parties that 'We are here until Friday, and I am certainly sitting next week, although in a different constitution.' Despite his haste, the eventual hearing was held in late-October, a few weeks into the next court term, again by the same three judges as had sat on the previous hearings.

The Lord Chief Justice's apparent desire both for consistency in the bench and speed differs from his approach to the proceedings (discussed in *Chapter One*) concerning the jury foreperson who may have known and signalled the victims' family. In that case, he presided over ordering the inquiry in May 1994, but the eventual hearing was held in 1995 before a completely different set of judges.

Lord Taylor's constant companions on the bench for Young's appeal were Sir Rodger Bell (a newly appointed judge, who would later become famous for presiding over the 1997 'McLibel' trial) and Sir Ronald Waterhouse (then in his final years on the bench and simultaneously running, for the first time, the International Eisteddfod, held in Wales in the second week of July). The latter's posthumous memoir described Taylor as 'a very dear and much admired friend', recounting how the pair first sat together as judges in 1985, enjoying pre-breakfast swims and judicial companionship. The memoir also labels *R v Young* 'the most bizarre appeal that I sat on', adding:

> We had little hesitation in concluding that there had been a material irregularity and that there was a real danger that what had happened in the Ouija session might have influenced some jurors. We therefore allowed the appeal and ordered a retrial. The whole episode had the flavour of a television play rather than a real-life (and very grave) criminal trial.

Beyond the evidence

> Although many, perhaps most, people would regard attempts to communicate with the dead as futile, there can be no doubt that the four jurors were going through the motions of asking questions to that end and apparently receiving answers.

Peter Taylor's court was not the first to assess the utility (rather than the tax classification) of Ouija boards. In 1958, Connecticut's Supreme Court considered a will that Helen Dow Peck, a wealthy widow 'of literary knowledge and artistic tastes', made when she was 71, 14 years before she died. After providing for her debts and gifts to two servants, she bequeathed the remainder of her $158,000 estate as follows:

> Third: I give, devise and bequeath to John Gale Forbes all the rest, residue and remainder of my estate, real, personal and mixed of whatsoever name and nature and wheresoever situated.

> Fourth: If the said John Gale Forbes be deceased, I direct that my estate be liquidated in part or whole as my executors may determine and the sum be reinvested and the income applied toward the investigation of telepathy among the insane for their understanding and cure. This sum is to be known as The John Gale Forbes Memorial Fund.

Alas, the executor was unable to locate Forbes and it turned out that Peck had never actually met him:

> In 1919, the testatrix had purchased a ouija board which she used with her husband. She told a friend sometime after 1940 that she played with this board and 'John Gale Forbes resolved out of space.' Through the board he became her correspondent, and she believed him to exist although she had never seen him.

The Supreme Court upheld the trial court's finding that 'John Gale Forbes was an imaginary person who had never existed' and 'that he was the product of a mental delusion, a monomania, which obsessed the testatrix prior to and in 1941 when she executed her will'. It ruled that Peck's entire will, including the gifts to her servants and the memorial fund, was void, allowing her surviving nieces and nephews to claim the estate.

Rejecting the possibility of life after death certainly makes it much easier to rule on the effect of a will. Oddly, though, Stephen Young's appeal could have been much more easily resolved if the court had accepted that the four jurors really did speak with Harry Fuller's ghost. Young's counsel argued that the hotel room séance was a 'material irregularity' in three ways:

> First, it was an attempt to acquire further evidence or information beyond the evidence in the case. Secondly or alternatively, Mr. Penry-Davey submits that what occurred was in the nature of an experiment which, as indicated above, cannot be countenanced. Thirdly, on any view of what occurred, only a third of the jury was present, so that matters relevant to the case took place when the jurors were not all together.

If the hotel room jurors actually did speak with the deceased, then each of these arguments would guarantee a new trial. The legal difficulty would be the same if the four jurors had uncovered non-paranormal messages from Harry, such as finding a note in his clothes in the jury room, or perhaps hearing a hidden message from him on the answering machine tape mentioning his worries about his insurance broker. The main problem in each instance is that Young's lawyers would have had no opportunity to respond to the implications of such significant information. And the trial judge would not have been able to rule on the evidence's admissibility or direct the jury on how it could be used. And, if they weren't present, nor could the other eight jurors properly debate the worth of the new discoveries.

A good example of such difficulties arose four years after Young's appeal. In a Bristol trial of charges that the defendant handled three stolen tyres, his defence was that he had purchased them recently. The jury sent the trial judge the following note:

> One of the jurors is a tyre specialist. The code 088 on the tyre signifies that the tyre was manufactured in the eighth week of 1998. The defendant claims to have had the tyres in his house around this period — certainly very little time for the tyres to have gone through normal purchase before being acquired by the defendant. May we take this into consideration?

While the trial judge and counsel were debating how to respond to this question, the jury returned with a guilty verdict. The Court of Appeal said that the trial judge should have instantly declared a mistrial, holding:

> It was not improper for a juror who was not a lawyer and who had specialist knowledge of circumstances forming the background to a particular case to draw upon that specialised knowledge in interpreting the evidence. However that knowledge was not to be used as evidence but as a means of considering, weighing-up and assessing the evidence before the court.

The difference between using knowledge as evidence and using it to interpret is certainly a subtle one, but there is no doubt that drawing on Harry's words from the after-life would fall on the wrong side of this line. Of course, the Court of Appeal was never going to find that the hotel room jurors actually spoke to Harry, but neither did it find that they didn't.

An awkward decision

> It seems to us that what matters is not whether the answers were truly from the deceased, but whether the jurors believed them to be so or whether they may have been influenced by the answers received during this exercise or experiment.

The court's holding that it didn't matter either way whether the four jurors spoke with Harry Fuller makes sense at first blush. The question of whether an irregularity is 'material' depends on what the jurors believe, not whether those beliefs are true or even rational. But, by removing the link between the jurors' conduct and reality, the Court of Appeal's approach significantly broadens what can count as an 'irregularity', allowing the jurors' mere thoughts to overturn a conviction.

On the day after Young's appeal was allowed, senior law lecturer Gary Slapper described the problem in a column in *The Times*:

> But suppose the jurors in the hotel had sought advice from their god through prayer? Would such a course of action invalidate their decision? They would, after all, be consulting something non-corporeal and something other than the evidence in the case. The divine and 'superstitious' oracles both rely on the faith of the juror.
>
> Will the Court of Appeal be able to argue, when its reasons are eventually given, that consulting a god for guidance is permissible but that consulting any other non-corporeal entity is not allowed? The court could avoid such a quandary by saying that absolutely nothing must guide jurors other than the evidence given in court. That option, however, would prevent religious people from receiving divine guidance when many must often be in great need of it. This would be an awkward decision from judges with the courts' motto Dieu et mon droit on a shield above them.

An American court (with 'In God We Trust' on its wall) was required to make exactly that awkward decision six years earlier.

In 1986, Tom DeMille became the first person in Utah to be convicted of murdering a child in his care, based on evidence of the child's extensive injuries before he was taken to a hospital emergency room. However, a juror later swore an affidavit that another juror told the rest that she had prayed about the case. Specifically:

> ...that while the defendant's attorney was giving his closing argument, she prayed, '...that if said attorney made eye-contact with her she would know he was telling the truth, but if he did not she would know he was not telling the truth about defendant; that he did not make eye-contact with her, so she knew said attorney was not telling the truth,' concerning the defendant...Said juror...was one of the leaders, during the deliberations by the jury, of the faction seeking a speedy and early determination of guilt of the defendant.

In 1988, a majority of Utah's Supreme Court dismissed DeMille's appeal. They held that upholding the defendant's complaint would amount to 'implicitly...holding that it is improper for a juror to rely upon prayer, or supposed responses to prayer, during deliberations', something they said would breach Utah's constitutional right to freedom of conscience. Only one judge would have ordered an inquiry on the ground that:

> ...if jurors were to agree that a verdict would be based on a 'divine sign,' a Ouija board answer, or some fortuitous event, such a verdict, in my judgement, would constitute a denial of due process and the right to trial by jury...The majority fails to draw a critical distinction between the legitimacy of jurors' seeking divine assistance in accurately and dispassionately weighing the evidence and the illegitimacy of jurors' abdicating their sworn duty to decide the case on the evidence and instead relying on some supposedly divine sign.

The difficult questions raised by such cases are not limited to spiritual matters. The problem in DeMille's case (though not the constitutional angle) would also have arisen if the juror had come up with her theory about the defence counsel's eye-contact by reading a book on pop psychology (or, for that matter, recalling a parent's advice, or a movie scene, or a university lecture, or her own specialist experience).

The Utah Supreme Court majority argued that personal beliefs, including irrational ones, are simply part of the jury system:

> The affidavit submitted in this case does not aver facts that would disqualify any juror. At most, it suggests that one juror may have been personally influenced by her own 'revelation' and that she told others of her experience as one means of persuading them to her point of view. This is certainly not an illegitimate inter-juror dynamic.

Six years later, the English Court of Appeal reached the opposite conclusion:

> Is Mr Lawson right in saying that what occurred was no different from jurors influencing each other? There is, in our view, a clear distinction between the views of one juror however strongly expressed, intended to influence others, and on the other hand revelations purporting to come from outside the jury and to be invested with some external authority however specious.

But the court did not spell out what, apart from Ouija boards, could be 'revelations purporting to come from outside the jury and ... invested with some external authority'. Prayer? Something a juror read in a book? Or saw on TV? Or was told by a friend? Or learnt from her work?

Or simply believed for whatever reason? The closest English courts have come to examining this question was a Newcastle trial in 1998, when a juror sent the trial judge a note asking for the defendant's date of birth, for use in determining his star sign. According to a court official, after the trial judge dismissed the juror from the panel, the juror:

> ...stood his ground and asked why. He seemed genuinely surprised he was being removed. He had been warned by the judge, as all jurors are, to try the defendants only on the evidence put before them in court.

While the trial judge was certainly right to refuse the juror's request for evidence that was not before the court, the juror was right to question why he was being dismissed. He surely isn't the only juror to believe in astrology (and others will often legitimately learn the defendant's birth date as part of the evidence). The remaining jurors acquitted the (Cancerian) defendant of violent disorder.

When dealing with people who believe in the supernatural, courts often suspect manipulation by a cynical third party. On 7th March 1930 in Buffalo, 66-year-old Nancy Bowen knocked at the door of Clothilde Marchand, a woman she barely knew, and beat her to death with a hammer. She later explained that her deceased husband had spoken to her via Ouija board, telling her the name of his killer and directing her to:

> …go to 576 Riley Street. It's a little house in the rear. She is short. Her hair is black with gray. It is bobbed. She has some teeth out—upper teeth. She has a police dog.

The police arrested not only Bowen but also her Ouija board partner, Lila Jimerson, who was having an affair with Clothilde's husband, Henri. After a 'Trial of the Century' (one of several in the USA that decade), Bowen was imprisoned for just one year and Jimerson was acquitted completely, apparently because the public came to blame Henri Marchand, a noted sculptor (who had speedily re-married, this time to his 18-year-old niece) for beguiling two credulous women into disposing of his wife.

The Court of Appeal never voiced the possibility that one of the four hotel room jurors—most obviously foreperson Ray, the only one of the quartet to claim any prior experience using Ouija boards—had used the incident to manipulate more credulous members of the panel. If there was such manipulation, its goal was not murder, but rather only a murder verdict. Of course, none of the jurors admitted convicting Young on the basis of what the Ouija board said. To the contrary, the court conceded that the participants all described the incident as a 'joke', hence the prosecution's argument:

The Ouija Board Jurors

This was, says Mr Lawson, no more than a drunken game and the court ought not to consider that it could have had any practical effect on the case. Nothing that happened, it was submitted, fell outside the scope of influences which jurors can properly bring to bear on one another.

How the Court of Appeal responded to that claim would decide the case's outcome.

The heart of the case

> Was it merely a drunken game which the court should disregard, as Mr. Lawson suggests? We do not think it can be laughed off in that way.

In the USA, jurors decide not only guilt or innocence, but also (in capital cases) life or death. Two weeks before Young's jury was empanelled, Colorado's Robert Harlan committed a horrific crime that would give pause to even the firmest opponents of capital punishment. He abducted a woman from a car park; raped her; drove by, shot and paralysed the driver of a car the woman escaped to; and then re-abducted the woman and killed her. Harlan's death sentence by a unanimous jury was upheld by the State Supreme Court in 2000, although the judges voiced some concerns about how his jury was selected. Five years later, new evidence led the court to revisit Harlan's case. Due to the enormous local publicity about Harlan's alleged crimes, his jury had been sequestered in a hotel and was not permitted access to either televisions or telephones. It turned out that several jurors spent their only night of deliberations reading the one diversion available to them.

After an investigation by Harlan's appeal team, one of the jurors later testified:

Q. When you resumed your deliberations the following morning, did you bring a Bible into the deliberation room with you?

A. Yes, I did.

Q. For what purpose?

A. To show Jesus the scriptures I had looked up.

Q. Did you show that to Jesus before a decision was made?

A. Yes.

The scriptures the juror marked were Leviticus 24:20-21 ('fracture-for-fracture, eye-for-eye, tooth-for-tooth. As he has injured the other, so he is to be injured. Whoever kills an animal must make restitution, but whoever kills a man must be put to death') and Romans 13:1 ('Let every soul be subject to the governing authorities for there is no authority except from God and the authorities that exist are appointed by God'). The 'Jesus' she showed the passages to was not the Christian Messiah but rather a fellow juror, Jesus Cordova.

The majority judgement of the Supreme Court of Colorado analysed this incident at length:

> The Leviticus text is written in the first person voice of God and commands death as the punishment for murder. The Romans text instructs human beings to obey the civil government. Here, the State of Colorado was seeking the death penalty. If the jury was unable to reach a unanimous verdict of death, the trial court would have been required to impose a life sentence without the possibility of parole. Drawn from an array of typical jurors in Colorado, at least one juror in this case could have been influenced by these authoritative passages to vote for the death penalty when he or she may otherwise have voted for a life sentence…
>
> The written word persuasively conveys the authentic ring of reliable authority in a way the recollected spoken word does not. Some jurors may view biblical texts like the Leviticus passage at issue here as a factual representation of God's will. The text may also be viewed as a legal instruc-

tion, issuing from God, requiring a particular and mandatory punishment for murder. Such a 'fact' is not one presented in evidence in this case and such a 'legal instruction' is not the law of the state or part of the court's instructions...

In a community where 'Holy Scripture' has factual and legal import for many citizens and the actual text introduced into the deliberations without authorization by the trial court plainly instructs mandatory imposition of the death penalty, contrary to state law, its use in the jury room prior to the penalty phase verdict was prejudicial to Harlan. Our analysis of the six factors for prejudice, in the context of a death penalty verdict, leads us to conclude that there is a reasonable possibility that the extraneous biblical texts influenced the verdict to Harlan's detriment.

The majority quashed the jury's death penalty, meaning that Harlan literally owes his life (in prison) to a *Gideon's Bible*.

The Colorado Supreme Court's decision was a controversial one, even prompting a petition for the recall of the majority judges. The minority judges emphasised the moral judgement that jurors in capital cases are required to make and the conflicting testimony from the jurors themselves, eight years after the deliberations, about the role (if any) that the biblical passages played in their deliberations. What is most notable, though, is the length and detail of the court's discussion. The judges were unanimous that the question of whether the jurors' potential consideration of extraneous material required quashing their verdict turned on six factors:

(1) how the extraneous information relates to critical issues in the case; (2) how authoritative is the source consulted; (3) whether a juror initiated the search for the extraneous information; (4) whether the information obtained by one juror was brought to the attention of another juror; (5) whether the information was presented before the jury reached a unanimous verdict; and (6) whether the information would be likely to influence a typical juror to the detriment of the defendant.

In Young's appeal, the Court of Appeal made an express finding about just the first of these factors:

> We stress that the answers which upset the jurors went to the heart of the case. They purported to deal with points which had been expressly raised by the evidence and they were strongly adverse to the appellant.

While the jurors' affidavits also clearly established the fifth factor listed by the Colorado court, and (probably) the third and fourth, the Court of Appeal made no findings at all about the second and sixth.

Rather, the court's rejection of the 'drunken game' scenario posited by the prosecution, and the jurors' own insistence that the incident was a 'harmless prank', drew on two pieces of evidence found by the Treasury Solicitor's investigation. Unwittingly echoing Parker Brothers' marketing tagline for its Ouija boards, the court wrote:

> The three women jurors were upset about what emerged. One was crying and took the view that it had gone too far. Why, if it was just a game? And why, when the verdict had been unanimous, should one juror (not one of the four) have been sufficiently concerned to consult a solicitor and make a statement about what had happened?

The Court of Appeal's analysis of these two questions was limited to posing them rhetorically. This book will reconsider each in its final two chapters.

The greatest Lord Chief Justice

> Having considered all the circumstances, we concluded there was a real danger that what occurred during this misguided ouija session may have influenced some jurors and may thereby have prejudiced the appellant. For those reasons we allowed the appeal but ordered a retrial.

According to the *Courier*, 'a woman sitting at the back of the court sobbed' as the Lord Chief Justice announced Stephen Young's retrial. Eighteen months later, Peter Taylor disclosed that he was suffering from a brain tumour and would cease judicial work and resign once a replacement was named. Following Taylor's final speech in Parliament that May, Lord Lester said he believed that Taylor 'will be recognised by future generations as the greatest Lord Chief Justice of this century'. Obituaries in April 1997 feted him for his unpretentious manner, his stand against mandatory sentencing and for raising English criminal justice from its early-1990s nadir.

The obituaries were unanimous that his career peaked before his appointment as Lord Chief Justice. In his 1990 report into the deaths of dozens of football spectators at Hillsborough stadium, Taylor, in defiance of the views of Margaret Thatcher, exonerated the fans and pilloried the police (some senior members of which by 2017 were facing prosecutions after charges were laid by the Crown Prosecution Service). His widely-implemented recommendation for seating in all soccer stadiums earned him the unofficial title 'Lord Football' and perhaps even his appointment as head of England's courts shortly after Thatcher's and Lane's downfalls. The Hillsborough Report was especially notable for its direct and eloquent prose:

> The police measures have worked to prevent violent outbursts in and around the ground. But at what a price! In addition to the poor facilities I described earlier (which are often worse for away than for home fans) the ordinary law-abiding football supporter travelling away is caught up in a police operation reminiscent of a column of prisoners of war being marched

and detained under guard…There is force too in the view that if people are herded and confined as potential offenders, that concept may in some cases become self-fulfilling.

Alas, such clear and compelling language was absent in the Court of Appeal's Ouija board judgement, which none of Taylor's obituaries mentioned. As will be discussed in *Chapter Five*, the judgement in Young's appeal has aged poorly since 1994. Nor has Lord Lester's prediction about Taylor's time as Lord Chief Justice been vindicated to date.

Six years after Taylor's death, the February 2003 episode of *Crimewatch* revealed that the West Yorkshire Police had obtained an unknown man's DNA profile from the clothes of stabbed eleven-year-old Lesley Molseed, fortuitously recovered from tape lifts made 30 years earlier. Four years later, Ronald Castree, the man who matched the DNA profile, was convicted of Molseed's murder. As with Stefan Kiszko before him, the guilty verdict was reached by a 10:2 majority and Castree continues to maintain his innocence. Also like Kiszko, his first appeal was rejected by the Court of Appeal, this time dismissing as speculation his claim that the incriminating DNA match was the result of contamination. All these revelations came over a decade after Kiszko's death by heart attack, 18 months after his release and six months before the passing of his mother Charlotte.

Cases such as Kiszko's leave no doubt that English criminal justice can produce miscarriages of justice even in non-terrorism or gang matters. Is Young's case a further example? The narration of the Ouija board case continues, this time from Young himself:

As I went into the kitchen, I called out 'Harry'. As I went further into the kitchen, looking through to the corridor, I could see there appeared to be a body or legs on the floor.

The Ouija Board Jurors

CHAPTER 4

Iceman

Imagine the shock — Smile of a killer — The bullets I had sold — Operation Arrowhead — Ali the Baddie — As if nothing had happened — Gun cupboard

Before the hotel room jurors turned to Harry Fuller, they first used their makeshift Ouija board to 'converse' with — as the Court of Appeal put it — 'persons known or related to two of the jurors (*one of them* being deceased)'. The court's potted explanation of talking boards claimed that they are used to 'seek messages from the spirits of *absent* or deceased persons'. In the past, Ouija board users have sometimes discovered, much to their embarrassment, that their purported interlocutors are alive. Presumably unaware of such incidents — or perhaps following the approach of Helen Peck Dow (discussed in *Chapter 3*) — the hotel room jurors apparently deliberately held a séance with at least one *living* person.

The Court of Appeal, uninterested in the events before the jurors purported to interrogate the undoubtedly dead Harry, didn't inquire further into this progenitor to text messaging (still a year away from public use in England in 1994). Mysteries abound. Why would a juror wish to commune with a living acquaintance or relative, particularly with a group of relative strangers late at night? What was asked? What answers were received? Was the acquaintance thought to be a conscious participant? And could the Ouija board users choose to speak to anyone, even if the recipient wasn't willing? Could they even have chosen to (purport to) speak with the one living person who knew the truth about whether Stephen Young killed the Fullers: Young himself?

At it happens, Young's first trial coincided with a vigorous debate in England about whether criminal suspects should be free to choose to remain silent when speaking with their investigators. The most controversial provisions of the new Criminal Justice and Public Order Bill introduced the month before Young's trial were ones permitting jurors to draw 'proper inferences' against defendants who didn't volunteer innocent accounts to their investigators in a timely way. But the new rules only became law in November 1994, so Young was free to stay silent, when questioned by both his investigators and his prosecutors. It didn't matter. The insurance broker spoke repeatedly to police about the events of February 10th 1993, each time bolstering the prosecution's case against him. He also testified in his own defence at both of his trials.

This chapter describes Young's various accounts, including his trial testimony, the centrepiece of the defence's argument that he was (and remains) wrongly convicted. What Young said at his trials would undoubtedly have dominated the deliberations of both juries that tried him, including the jury that spent the night at Brighton's *The Old Ship Hotel*.

Imagine the shock

> What really hit home with me, what scared me, was the fact that I had been in the vicinity roughly at the time this supposedly happened.

The Sussex Police first spoke to Stephen Young as just one of Harry Fuller's many acquaintances, which included his ex-wives, ex-girlfriends, family, in-laws, business associates, car sellers, car buyers, ex-criminals and current ones. On Monday 22nd February 1993, 12 days after the Fullers died and exactly a year before Adrian's jury was sworn in, Young spoke to PC Stephen Fulcher. He readily admitted to Fulcher that he had a murdered man as his client, but said that he had last spoken with Harry some five days before his death. That account, the first of at least three from Young, was disproved by the Geemarc answering machine the police found under a sofa in Blackmans Cottage, which contained a tape of Harry's recording of his final phone calls. Especially in an era without voicemail or smartphones, it would surely have shocked the insurance broker to hear his private conversation with a dead man broadcast on national television.

Young's second contact with the Sussex Police was by letter—two typed pages that he delivered in person to the Fuller investigation's headquarters in East Grinstead, two days after the *Crimewatch* broadcast and exactly one year before news broke of the Ouija board incident. Young's letter contradicted part of what he had told the police eight weeks earlier. He now admitted to phoning Harry on the evening of Tuesday 9th February to arrange a meeting the next morning to discuss selling an acquaintance's Porsche. An early morning house call for this purpose might be difficult to credit, but Young's new claim was of course corroborated by Harry's recording of the pair's conversation. That conversation also showed that Young had recently tried to visit the cottage at night, seemingly without prior arrangement, but also without any apparent objection or surprise from Harry.

Young's letter also set out his first version of events in Wadhurst on the morning of 10th February 1993. Admitting his presence there, he said that he arrived late to the Wednesday morning appointment thanks to roadworks, estimating that he knocked at the door of Blackmans Cottage at 8.20. The curtains were drawn and 'I thought it obvious they were not even up. I went to the door. There was no reply'. After wandering on the high street to kill time:

> I thought I would give it one more try. There was no reply again. I thought I would push-off. Off I trotted. Then, of course, on Thursday I heard what had happened.

He wrote that he was gone by 8.40, adding: 'When I heard what had happened, you can imagine the shock I felt. I had not heard or seen anything'. The timing he gave had the broker knocking at the dealer's door ten minutes either side of Harry's brief trip to Goble's tobacconist, described on *Crimewatch* two days earlier.

Why didn't Young tell the investigators this earlier? He said that he did ring at one point to see if the police wanted to interview him but:

> ...the chap said: 'No, you will be contacted in due course.' I didn't want to get involved in it. I didn't know what sort of thing he had got himself into. I was a little apprehensive that if it came out that I might have been a witness or may have seen something...I was a little concerned for my safety.

This scarcely explains why he told what seem to be outright lies to the police when they did speak to him 12 days after the murders. One of the interviewing detectives told Young: 'I found it a little bit curious—obviously you are a law-abiding person—that it's been nine weeks for you to come to us'. The broker's response: 'I had not seen anything or heard anything that I thought would be of assistance'.

With every word, Young was now greatly assisting the police (and his later prosecutors, who played the tape of the police interview to the jury). Had he read the *Kent and Sussex Courier* four weeks after Harry's death, he would have seen, at the foot of an article announcing a £10,000 reward for information, the following update on the ongoing investigation:

> Some of the 50 officers still working on the case have been studying video pictures taken by a security camera in the lobby of Lloyds Bank next to a cashpoint, close to the cottage, between 8.30 and 9 am on February 10. This is helping to build a pattern of the people and vehicles going through that part of the High Street when it is thought the murders were committed.

The small strip of houses and shops that included Blackmans Cottage happened to be opposite both of Wadhurst's banks and their CCTV cameras, which is how the police knew exactly when Harry made his final shopping trip at 8.33 am, which took the dealer past Lloyd Bank's security camera. The same camera showed Young's customised white VW Golf arriving in Wadhurst at 8.03 am and departing at 9.09 am, more than enough time to shoot the Fullers after Harry returned from buying the newspaper and before Nicola left for her temporary work in Tunbridge Wells. Both sides in the trial accepted that Young didn't appreciate how readily his actions could be tracked by fixed cameras, a sign of simpler times before England became the world's leader in CCTV.

The bank camera evidence completed the prosecution's case that Young had the means (his arsenal), motive (his debts and Harry's cash) and opportunity (his presence in Wadhurst) to kill the Fullers. Combined with his changing story and the similar bullets found at his home and the crime scene, the prosecution's case, while wholly circumstantial, was very strong. It was obvious that Young's only real hope of an acquittal was to take the stand at his trial.

Smile of a killer

> A man answered the phone. I believe it was Harry. I said: 'I'm parked out the back'. He said: 'I'll be down, give me 15 minutes'.

The media has two photos of Stephen Young, both grainy images of him in a dark suit smiling at the camera, each obviously cropped from a larger photo. Especially when contrasted — as it often was in newspapers — with Harry's loud grin and Nicola's delight as the couple cut their wedding cake, Young's expression in each photo, like most people's in such shots, seemed posed. Following his conviction, the media labelled it, meaninglessly, the 'Smile of a Killer'. It is unlikely that he was smiling, genuinely or otherwise, as he testified at his two murder trials, where he confirmed both of his previous accounts to the police were lies.

Well, partial lies. His trial account still had him arriving late to his appointment at Blackmans Cottage (albeit only by a few minutes) and receiving no answer when he knocked at the door: 'Both sets of curtains, upstairs and downstairs, were closed. I stood back and waited. Nothing happened'. As per his letter, Young said that he wandered past Wadhurst's shops to kill time and still received no response when he knocked again. But, he now admitted, his attempt to phone the car dealer's mobile succeeded (consistently with phone records that showed a brief call between the pair's mobiles at 8.10 am, something he also hadn't mentioned in his letter to the police). A man's voice, seemingly just roused from sleep, told him to wait.

While Young wasn't sure that the man he spoke to was Harry, the timing of this conversation is consistent with the recipient being the car dealer, matching both his reputation as a late riser and the CCTV images showing him stepping out for cigarettes and papers just after 8.30 am. Young now claimed that these were Harry's last words to his broker. The alleged conversation helped explain the lengthy period Young spent in Wadhurst for an appointment that never actually happened. The broker said that he waited in his car for a while and then returned to the front of the house. Again, there was no response but this time a curtain had been opened. Figuring Harry may be waiting in the rear car park, Young walked there to find the cottage's back door ajar.

Now Young added his most dramatic claim: he was the first person to discover the very crime he was accused of committing. After describing seeing legs through the door (much like Nicola's parents would later that day), he told the jury:

> I recognised it as Harry. I went over and there was no sign of movement. I assumed he had had a heart attack or collapsed. I tried his pulse three times but couldn't find anything. I tried to re-position him. There was blood which appeared to be coming from his nose or mouth area. He was obviously dead.

With that claim, Young joined the unfortunate ranks of criminal defendants who (belatedly) admitted to having stumbled onto terrible crimes that they didn't report until after suspicions fell upon them. In such cases, jurors are invited to accept the possibility that the defendant was merely an exceptionally poor citizen, rather than a criminal one.

The main virtue of Young's new account for the defence — that it now fitted the other timing evidence gathered by the police — was mixed, because it also fitted the prosecution's narrative of the broker's repeated attempts to avoid detection for the murders. Michael Lawson's theory was that Young initially thought that he had got away with a perfect crime — after all, no-one in Wadhurst reported seeing him in the village at all — only to be foiled by two types of unforeseen surveillance: Harry's recording of his own calls and the bank's CCTV, respectively disproving the broker's first two accounts of the events of 10th February. It later emerged that Young first told his solicitors his third version of events at Lewes Prison on 28th June 1993, over two months after his arrest and, crucially, *after* he had been given the committal papers containing the evidence that contradicted his earlier account. The jury could clearly have drawn a very negative inference against the broker from this sequence of events.

By presenting his new version of the events of that Wednesday morning, Young therefore took on two additional burdens. The first was to account for his repeated decisions to lie to the Sussex Police. The second was to convincingly explain away the other circumstantial evidence that linked him to the Fullers' deaths, notably the matching bullets found at his house. In his trial testimony, Young added a new story that purported to explain away both of these problems.

The bullets I had sold

> I just put two and two together very quickly and presumed he had been shot with a gun I sold him a month before.

Most people who stumble onto a murder will focus either on the victim or the potential villains. But Stephen Young said that his attention quickly fell on a bullet cartridge case lying beside the car dealer's corpse. Here, the broker's account took a liability for the defence — the defendant's 'obsession' with guns — and turned it into something of a positive. The prosecution had already shown the jury a 15 minute video on how gun enthusiasts like Young make their own bullets. So, Young could plausibly testify that he instantly recognised that the cartridge case next to Harry Fuller was from a .32 bullet, the sort used in a Walther PPK. He explained that this was a weapon he knew well.

At his trial, Young publicly admitted for the first time having purchased a replica Walther PPK in 1988, some five years before the murders. As discussed in *Chapter 2,* he purchased the gun from dealers in Little Eaton. This purchase explained why the broker had plenty of ammunition for such a gun in his house and office, but it also all but confirmed that the Fullers were indeed killed with a gun owned by the man charged with their murder. Unsurprisingly, Young's admission came with an innocent, but complex, explanation for this very suspicious circumstance. According to him, Harry had once asked his broker: 'Can you get hold of any clean guns?' A month before he died, Harry and a stranger appeared at the office of Young and Harding Associates on Pembury's high street. According to Young, the car dealer said he wanted a pistol or a revolver. I asked him what he wanted it for. He said: "Protection".'

Harry's alleged answer was what anyone seeking a gun in such circumstances would say, but it was also entirely consistent with the prosecution's case that the car dealer feared for his and Nicola's safety. Likewise, his broker's position as a senior gun club member (not to mention a hoarder of illicit weapons) made him a natural recipient for such a request. According to Young, his conversation with Harry and his unidentified colleague moved on to choosing a weapon for the car dealer. Offered either a Browning 9 mm pistol or a replica Walther PPK, Harry chose the latter, effectively, on the defence's account, selecting the weapon that would soon kill him and his wife. The dealer allegedly bought the weapon and 30 or 40 rounds of Young's custom-made ammunition for £150, cash that, on the prosecution's case, would have been very handy to Young. Young claimed that this was the same encounter where the two first spoke about Harry buying a Porsche from an associate of Young's, the prelude to the arrangement that would bring the broker to Blackmans Cottage on 10th February 1993.

Not only did Young's new story explain the link between the bullets in his house and those used to kill the Fullers, but it also accounted for his failure to report Harry's murder to the police. Sitting in his own car outside Blackmans Cottage, he told the jury, he dialled 999 but then thought twice:

> Having spoken to Harry half an hour earlier, and then found him dead with one of the bullets I had sold him with the gun, I started to think: 'I don't want to get involved in this'. I didn't put the call through.

In short, Young said that he feared that his many innocent links to Harry's death — his presence at the crime scene at around the time of the murder and his purchase of the gun that killed the couple, and perhaps also his money problems — would inevitably be seen by the police as extremely suspicious. The prosecution case presented at Young's trial naturally bore out that very logic.

But Young's new tale had two obvious flaws. The first was that it was clearly possible that the broker had invented his sale of the gun to Harry as the only way to explain the circumstantial case against him. As the Court of Appeal would later point out, Young's admission to his lawyer that he had purchased the weapon (made on 28th June 1993, the same day he revealed to his solicitor that he saw Harry's corpse) came after he:

> …had first had the opportunity to look at the committal papers, which tied the bullets at the cottage to the bullets which had been found at his (the appellant's) house.

The second flaw is that it is unclear how Harry came to be shot with a gun that, by Young's account, the dealer purchased for his own protection. Young, of course, didn't claim to know, saying only that, 'I thought that there had been an argument and at that stage Nicola had even shot him'. This scenario was disproved by Nicola's corpse in the upper floor of Blackmans Cottage, which Young insisted he never saw.

At Young's trials, the defence speculated that Harry may have drawn the weapon in an attempt to defend himself from his assailant and then was somehow disarmed, allowing his attacker to use the weapon to kill the couple. As the judge explained to Young's jury at his second trial, this theory has any number of plausibility problems:

> Harry Fuller is shot in the back. How does he get hold of the gun and is able to shoot him with the barrel of the gun only a short distance away

from his back at the time he fired it if it was Harry Fuller who had the gun? Somehow or other he must have got it from Harry Fuller. If it was a fight but [of] which there is no indication at all and there was a fight, why then surely Nicola Fuller would have run downstairs to see what had happened instead of apparently not doing that from where she was shot, if that is the proper deduction. Does it mean that Harry Fuller showed the gun, he said look and takes it from him loaded and shoots him, although by chance he actually has come there to kill him which means he must have had another weapon in his own pocket but he prefers to use Harry Fuller's gun. You must work all this out by yourself.

But there was one necessary element of this story — the existence of someone other than Young with a reason to kill Harry — that was entirely plausible.

Operation Arrowhead

> I then heard some movement above me. It sounded like a clump, like somebody walking.

Stephen Young's innocent account naturally implied, indeed necessitated, that someone else killed the car dealer while Young unknowingly waited outside. This was presumably the person who Young heard walking around upstairs as he examined Harry's body and the bullet that killed him. Naturally, Young didn't investigate further — 'I basically panicked. I just turned and went out as quickly as I could'. But, he said, he saw a man's face 'either balding or with very fair hair, at the attic window'. Young did not claim to know who that man was.

The goal that the prosecution said motivated Young — his need for quick cash — by no means ruled out others with a similar motive, especially given broad knowledge of Flash Harry's money habits in his circle. Indeed, one of the main weaknesses of the prosecution case was that the police could not find any reason for Young to kill Harry other than a need for quick cash. Even the jurors' Ouija board—which had been ready to speculate on where the gun and excess cash had ended up—couldn't produce an additional motive for killing Harry, much less one for killing Nicola too. If, as the prosecution argued, Young's sole motive for killing Nicola was to avoid her identifying him as her husband's killer, then why didn't he arrange to meet Harry when his wife was at work (or dining, as she had been the night before her death) seven miles away in Tunbridge Wells? Indeed, why didn't he simply burgle Blackmans Cottage while both of the Fullers were out, something their neighbours said was common enough and which Young was aware had occurred a few nights earlier? This particular crack in the prosecution case is significantly widened by abundant evidence, uncovered by the police investigation itself, of others who had motives well beyond money to kill Harry.

Initial care of the investigation was given to Detective Superintendent Brian Foster, head of East Sussex CID and nearing the end of a 30-year career in the police force. He would shortly leave to work for a victim support charity and then spend a decade investigating war crimes for the United Nations. In the investigation's early days, Foster told the media that angles he was pursuing included a 'love triangle' (given that Nicola was shot 'in the head') and notes left on both Harry's car ('Where are you, Harry? I've been trying to contact you' signed 'Tony') and Nicola's convertible (an abusive note related to a parking dispute). 'The crime bears all the hallmarks of a grudge killing', an unnamed detective told the media.

Within a few days, Detective Chief Inspector Alan Snelling was presented as the investigation's head. Snelling would also shortly leave the homicide branch to join the Sussex Police discipline and complaints department. He told the media that his preferred theory was a contract killing:

> The nature of the killings means the possibility that we are looking at a professional murder cannot be ruled out. The killer was certainly ruthless in the way he executed his crime.

Mere burglary, by contrast, didn't rate highly as a possible motive: 'The house had not been ransacked and whoever killed them did so in cold blood'. If the crime was due to a business deal with Harry, Snelling said, then the deal 'must have gone badly wrong'. He revealed that the investigation was not limited to Sussex, but was also exploring leads in Kent and London. Meanwhile, the *Daily Express* claimed that Harry had 'a lot of enemies, perhaps from rival gipsy clans'. After the 'disappointing' response to an offer of a £10,000 reward — twice the previous amount ever offered by the Sussex police — for information (including posters at car auctions through Sussex and Kent), Snelling told the press that he was keeping an open mind and wouldn't rule out a 'gangland connection'.

Three weeks after the Fullers' deaths, a third senior police officer, Detective Superintendent Graham Hill, wrote to all the households of Wadhurst describing himself as 'the Officer in overall charge of enquiries into the murders'. Hill told the media:

> This is a very big case, with lots of lines of inquiry. Now we are into the hard task of assessing all the information we have collected.

To pursue Harry's business dealings, the Sussex Police 'worked closely' with those from Kent and placed officers at Tunbridge Wells Police Station. Hill described some of the leads in the *Crimewatch* episode that helped to target Young. The BBC reconstruction quoted a postman who had been startled by a car suddenly departing from behind Blackmans Cottage at 6.30 on the morning of the Fullers' deaths:

> It's normally very quiet in the morning. The dirty blue Ford Escort pulled out in front of me which caught me by surprise. The passenger seemed 35 to 40, tall and well-built, and the vehicle travelled towards Tunbridge Wells.

The superintendent also asked viewers about another vehicle that was clearly not Young's white VW Golf:

> Just after eight that morning in the car park at the rear of Blackmans Cottage, a lady saw a long black-bonneted vehicle — something like a

Jaguar—pull up and a man get out of the vehicle and he was very distinctive in that he was wearing a long black coat, almost to the ground. We would like anyone else who saw that man or the vehicle to please make contact with us.

Hill remained on the Fuller case through both of Young's trials, by which time he had succeeded Foster as head of Sussex CID. He retired in 1996 after 28 years in the Sussex Police.

Clearly, Operation Arrowhead, the investigation of the Fullers' deaths, had many strands, which is unsurprising given the nature of the killings and Harry's circle. Little can be read into the media's reports of the investigation, which were doubtless carefully managed by the police and mixed genuine journalism with gossip. What is more important is the evidence implicating others in Harry's death that remained unresolved by the time of Young's trial. In his trial testimony, Hill conceded that he had pursued claims that Harry was dealing in either cannabis or cocaine; he said that he had never been able to establish the link and that the white powder found on Harry's body was sugar, suggesting an attempt to create a false lead. But he also confirmed widespread rumours that Harry had been a police informant who had revealed a car ringing operation. When Young's counsel suggested that this was an obvious motive for Harry to be killed by a criminal acquaintance (and, by implication, not his otherwise clean insurance broker), Hill could only speculate that Young may have chosen to target Harry in part because he had so many enemies.

Two leads the police pursued clearly went well beyond speculation. One involved Roger Lee, with whom Harry had had 'business dealings' and who the Court of Appeal would later describe as a violent man known to threaten people with shotguns. Five days before his death, Harry had told a police sergeant that he was having 'trouble' with Lee because of Lee's suspicions that the car dealer was the grass in a car ringing matter. In fact, Lee was the first man arrested on suspicion of killing the Fullers. During the trial, the media reported:

Mr Lee, who lived in a caravan in Coldharbour, near Maidstone, was quizzed by the officers a fortnight after the double murder. He answered 'no comment' to all the questions put to him in the interview, Det Con Marc Flannery told the jury at Hove Crown Court, Sussex. But Mr Lee was later ruled out of the inquiry by detectives who eventually charged 35-year-old insurance broker Stephen Young with the killings. Det Con Flannery said that Lee, who had a cocaine habit, 'appeared to like frightening people and inflicting pain on them'.

The police said that they released Lee after his mobile phone records indicated that he was well away from Wadhurst at the time of the deaths. Nevertheless, the defence adduced evidence that a Jaguar XJS similar to Lee's was caught on the Lloyds Bank CCTV on the Wednesday morning and that the 'gangster and Al Capone figure' had indeed lost money after Harry tipped-off police to a car-ringing gang.

A further, still more startling lead was a second answering machine that Harry used to record his calls and that was apparently kept under a different couch. Astonishingly, the final call on the Boots answering machine's tape contained what the Court of Appeal would later describe as a 'threat' to see Harry 'tomorrow morning'. The police soon identified the caller as Colin Gabriel, who had had a 'fight' with Harry in October 1992. Gabriel was never arrested. The Court of Appeal later gave a frustratingly slight explanation for the police's lack of interest:

> As far as that threat was concerned, the prosecution case was that it was the last message on a tape which related to a period in the autumn of 1992, that is October or November 1992, Gabriel having severed any connections with Harry Fuller by November 1992.

And yet, Nicola's mother testified that one of her own calls captured on the Boots machine tape was much more recent and an eye-witness told the jury that he saw Gabriel's Audi in Wadhurst on the day of the murders.

These various twists and unresolved loose ends are nothing unusual in a complex inquiry, and they certainly don't rule out Young's guilt. What they do show is that the Court of Appeal's summary of the case in its 1994 judgement (set out at the end of *Chapter 2*) was incomplete.

While the facts the court listed were indeed the matters the hotel room jurors addressed with their makeshift Ouija board, it is likely that they were only a background to the jury's real dilemma during its deliberations on 22nd and 23rd March 1994: whether the Fullers had been killed by one of the many potential criminals with a grudge against Harry, or by his insurance broker, an otherwise seemingly non-violent man who simply needed money. The deceased Harry (or whatever else moved the jurors' glass) offered no insight into this core puzzle beyond the bland confirmation that it was Young who killed both Harry and Nicola.

Ali the Baddie

> I was becoming muddled. I didn't really know what was happening and what had gone on.

What was it about Stephen Young that would lead him, rather than one of the car dealer's many enemies, to kill Harry and Nicola Fuller? At his first trial in February and March 1994, Young called witnesses to testify to his good character, but he chose not to do so in his retrial later that year. The Court of Appeal suggested why:

> One can only assume that he considered that the consequences of taking that course at the first trial had resulted in a significant tactical disadvantage because it enabled the prosecution to make a double play with, firstly, the way in which the appellant was behaving towards his creditors and, secondly, the circumstances in which the guns came to be both owned and modified and the ammunition treated in the way that it was.

By arguing in the first trial that the insurance broker was both believable and non-violent, the defence made it easier for the prosecution to introduce evidence to the contrary.

The prosecution evidence that Young wasn't believable included not only his earlier lies to the police (which were inevitably before the jury) but also evidence that he had operated his insurance brokerage dishonestly. Michael Lawson told the jury that Young 'had, over a number of years, been stealing commission monies belonging to insurance companies for whom he was an agent'. The Court of Appeal (apparently relying on admissions by Young at his trial) said that he used £40,000 of premiums paid by his clients to manage his debts instead of passing them on to the insurers. This evidence was especially damaging to the defence, as it provided a stronger imperative for Young to pay off his debts; bankruptcy would inevitably expose some of his underhanded conduct.

At his second trial, Young opted for a narrower stance on his supposed good character, merely asking the trial judge to tell the jury that his undoubted clean criminal record up to 1993 meant that they should look more sceptically at the prosecution case. However, even putting aside his insurance dealings, Young's repeated lies to the police meant that his record was no guarantee of his honesty. And his arsenal of weapons, including illegal ones, likewise robbed him of the argument that he had no criminal propensities. The Court of Appeal observed that the broker had admitted:

> ...the fact was that he was in possession of—and this was perhaps the most significant aspect of the story—at least two (and the evidence suggested significantly more) illicit firearms. By illicit, we mean not merely illicit in the sense that they were firearms which it was unlawful for him to have, but illicit in the sense that it is difficult to see what legitimate purpose he could have had for those firearms in the particular configuration in which they were, because the two which were most relevant, namely the Walther PPK and the Browning (that is the two about which more detail was heard than the rest), had been modified in ways that made it difficult to see how they could have been required for any sporting, target or other legitimate purpose.

Indeed, if Young's retrial had occurred a decade later, after England's laws on bad character evidence were liberalised, his jury could have used the mere fact of Young's possession of 'illicit' firearms as evidence that he was a potential killer.

Young's character was the topic of much discussion after his trial:

Tom Fuller, 40, one of Harry's six brothers, said yesterday : 'Young is evil and callous. This verdict is a great weight off our shoulders'.

Businessman Michael Johnson, Nicola's father, said: 'I think probably Young might be a psychopath. Young appears void of any emotion. The verdict doesn't change things for us at all. We can't bring Nicky back but this does take one evil person off the streets'.

Detective Chief Superintendent Graham Hill, who led the murder investigation, said: '…These were cold, callous and calculated murders and all the evidence is that they were pre-planned'.

Hill even thought it relevant that, as the media put it, 'Weeks before the murders, [Young] stole the show with his comic portrayal of Ali Baba in the village's Christmas panto'.

Since at least 1992, Young had been one of the Pembury Players, 'one of few [village] societies that cater for both sexes of all ages, shapes and sizes'. A year before the Fullers died, he appeared in *The Other Mother Goose* as 'one half of a double-act with his friend Stephen Murphy'. His role a year later, in an annual pantomime that played four times over three days in early January 1993, earned the following review in the *Pembury Village News*:

Traditional pantos need hisses and boos, a few flashes and a very bad baddie and Pembury Players' recent production of Ali the Baddie had all these and more, providing a good evening's entertainment to a packed Village Hall on 9 January. Steve Young's moustachioed Ali, and his baddies Paul Russell and David Cole had the audience booing and hissing from the very start, with Maggie Weaver's Aladdin making sure there were plenty of cheers to out-do him.

Young's wife Sally, who played the hag 'Ever Ready', sang a 'delightful rendition' of *Somewhere Out There*. The reviewer disagreed with Hill about who 'stole the show', awarding that title to Murphy (who wrote and directed *Ali the Baddie*, as well as taking on dual roles via quick wig changes after the actress playing Aladdin's girlfriend called in sick).

Hill's theory? That the annual Pembury pantomime was the inspiration for Young's own moustache-twirling murder plot.

As if nothing had happened

> I got a call at the office and the man said, 'You didn't see anything last week did you? It would be better for you, Sally and the boys if you didn't. Do we understand each other?'

One thing about Stephen Young always confounded his investigators. According to Hill:

> He had clearly thought through things and within an hour of the murders was talking perfectly normally to his business associates and wife.

Indeed, he kept an appointment that morning with an insurance representative, Martin Bell, where he signed a post-dated cheque for £6,000. Bell noticed nothing unusual, nor did members of the Freemasonry lodge where Young attended a meeting on the night of the murders 'as if nothing had happened'. Stephen Fulcher, the police constable who interviewed Young two weeks after the killings told his jury:

> He seemed entirely normal and relaxed. I was very surprised to hear later that he was implicated. From his demeanour he did not arouse my suspicions.

All of the broker's police interviews, including several days of interrogation following his arrest, were 'calm' and 'relaxed'.

Most people would expect a man who has just killed two people—especially a man who was unlikely to have ever killed before—to struggle to keep his composure, both after the killings and when later questioned. But the same expectation would also apply, perhaps more so, to a man who had come across a dead person, most likely killed by his own gun, and who then came to be suspected, and then accused, of a horrible crime he didn't commit. Young's behaviour was a poor fit to both the prosecution and defence narratives. Hill made the best of the situation, telling the media that Young's 'self-assured, level-headedness fitted perfectly the profile of the cool killer being hunted by the police'. He added 'We nicknamed him "Mr Cool"', describing the broker as 'the coolest and most cold-blooded criminal' he had met in his career. *Crimewatch*, in a 1996 retrospective feature on the Fuller case, adopted a variation: 'Iceman'.

These various portrayals of Young match both his alleged murders and his conduct after them. But they are also an all too convenient explanation for otherwise problematic parts of the prosecution case: that Young killed two people for little reason other than obtaining quick cash to clear some of his debts, and that he never confessed his crimes, despite the overwhelming evidence of his guilt. They also sit poorly with what else was known about him: that he was happily married, well-liked by his community and clients, and had no record for violence or (apart from his recent embezzling) dishonesty. Nor do they address several straightforward, unforced errors Young made, such as not recognising how the bank's CCTV would expose his second account of his actions and not disposing of the many .32 bullets he had in his house and workplace. Such incongruities in an investigation are common, of course, but they demonstrate the limits of the police's and media's pop psychology. The best prosecution theory seems to be that Young was Mr Cool some of the time and a mere fool for the rest of it.

For his part, Young offered a very different explanation for his unruffled demeanour between the Fullers' deaths and his being charged with their murder: his family's life depended upon it. He told the jury that he received several anonymous calls in the weeks after Harry's and Nicola's murders expressly naming and threatening his wife Sally and his two children. Asked if he 'understood' the caller's threat: 'I said I did and he just hung up. I didn't recognise the voice and the call scared me rigid'.

The Ouija Board Jurors

His theory was that the person upstairs at Blackmans Cottage saw Young leaving the house and recognised him. He added that he received two further calls that left him in no doubt that the threat was a real one, prompting him to carry a pistol: 'If there had been any trouble, I would have used it'. Of course, there was no proof of these claims of muted heroism beyond the broker's say-so.

Gun cupboard

> I'm innocent, I didn't do it, my Lord.

When Adrian's jury delivered its verdict, Young gently shook his head while his wife (and several jurors) sobbed and others in the court cheered, events that started Adrian on the road to exposing the Ouija board jurors. The broker has maintained his innocence ever since.

But few others see his conviction as troubling. The chief problem he faces is that, even on his own account, he is the victim of some extraordinary bad luck: that he happened to be in Wadhurst for an unusual appointment just as Harry and Nicola were killed, that he happened to have sold Harry the gun that was somehow used to kill them, and that he happened to be facing severe financial difficulties at the time, including a demand that came due that very morning, that could have been met by the cash seemingly taken from Blackmans Cottage. As well, he paid off some of that morning's debt in cash. Young offered no explanation for the latter fact other than coincidence: he insisted that he had been saving the cash for some time, keeping it in his 'gun cupboard in his home'. The sole support for that claim, apart from his say-so, was the jurors' makeshift Ouija board, which likewise claimed that the money was in a 'case'.

However, Young's appeal has since become emblematic of a particular risk of miscarriage of justice, one that is sourced from the jury system itself. The story of the Ouija board case is now eloquently narrated by its most prominent critic, Cambridge University's Professor John Rason Spencer, who wrote in 1995:

> What is extraordinary about this case is not the fact that the jurors used a ouija board, nor that the Court of Appeal quashed the conviction because they had done so. It is that it was, legally, an uphill task to get the conviction quashed on such a ground.

The Ouija Board Jurors

CHAPTER 5

Mansfield's Window

A delicate minuet — Outside of the door — The freedom to act irresponsibly — An embarrassing situation — Horror stories — The absurdities of life.

Two decades after the Fullers died, a jury trying economist Vicky Pryce for perverting the course of her politician husband's speeding fine asked the trial judge a series of questions. Such inquiries are the main window outsiders have into how juries deliberate. The questions the foreperson asked in Pryce's high-profile trial — including 'Can a juror come to a verdict based on a reason that was not presented in court and has no facts or evidence to support it either from the prosecution or defence?' — triggered another crisis of confidence in the English jury system.

The University of Cambridge responded by posting a YouTube video entitled 'The Defects of Jury Trials', where one of its professors declared that, 'though juries have their passionate defenders', they are slow, expensive and 'surprisingly accident prone':

> In 1995 there was a murder trial after which it was revealed that some of the jurors had sought to make contact with the spirit of the murder victim by using a Ouija board, on account of which the Court of Appeal had to quash the conviction and order a retrial at the end of which the new jury convicted without the benefit of spiritual intervention. There was the case in 1981 where, on the 12th day of a fraud trial, the judge had to discharge the jury because some young women on the jury had got drunk celebrating their 21st birthday during the lunch hour and were seen to be making sexual

advances to a male juror which, surprisingly perhaps, he was not at all happy with. Two years ago there was the 'Crapland' case as it was called, a prosecution [of] some fraudsmen for running a fraudulent Christmas site called 'Lapland', and hence its unattractive nickname, for which the conviction was eventually quashed when it was revealed that one of the jurors had been exchanging texts with her boyfriend in the public gallery in order to find all the things which they weren't supposed to hear that were happening when they were out.

Informing his YouTube audience that he had 'a file of these cases collected over many years and I could give a great many other examples', the professor suggested several solutions to the 'obvious problem of quality control': requiring people to apply for and be trained to be jurors; having lay jurors sit with judges; and making jurors provide reasons for guilty verdicts.

This was by no means a new stance for Professor John Spencer, then about to retire into an emeritus professorship. At the other end of his career in 1986, when he was a lecturer at the same university, he spent half of a review of a book on fraud law taking the authors to task for briefly praising the role juries play in fraud trials:

> The argument is clinched, with the intellectual rigour which so characterises public discussion about the merits of juries, by an anecdote about a jury in a fraud case who loved it so much they volunteered for second helpings, and a milkman juror who could do sums in his head quicker than counsel with the help of a calculator.

Spencer concluded by asking: 'Why do so many people, including distinguished academics and leading practitioners at the criminal Bar, keep puffing juries as the best bulwark against conviction of the innocent?'

Closer to the middle of his career, one year after the Court of Appeal allowed Young's appeal, Spencer published 'Séances and the Secrecy of the Jury-Room'. This was the first of several pieces he wrote that argued that the Ouija board case demonstrated a significant flaw in the law of juries. Spencer's close attention to the case is one reason why it continues to be discussed decades later. This chapter explains how the case became a poster child for criticisms of the law on jury secrecy and how a hypothetical Spencer posed about the case played an outsize role in both how the law later developed and how the Ouija board jurors have been misunderstood.

A delicate minuet

> The Crown first argued that the inquiry the Court of Appeal ordered was illegal, and then tried to say that it should not quash the conviction because of the results. And what is more, in so arguing, the Crown seemed to have the law on its side.

As the Court of Appeal heard Stephen Young's arguments in mid-1994, the English media reported that 'the case has presented the judges with a major constitutional headache because the Contempt of Court Act 1981 (see below) forbids anyone, even appeal judges, to probe into jury room secrets'. That headache's origin was in events 15 years earlier.

On 23rd July 1979, the *New Statesman* published the third in a series of post mortems on that decade's 'Trial of the Century', the prosecution of English politician Jeremy Thorpe for allegedly arranging his ex-lover's murder. The case's iconic status was tarnished by the supposed conspiracy's abject failure (only the target's dog, Rinka, was killed), the jury's acquittal of all involved and an ensuing debate about whether that outcome was due to pro-defence bias by the jury, the trial judge or the prosecution. The *New Statesman* promised an insight into the latter question:

> These arguments have been advanced, so far, into a vacuum: gaining force from the fact that convention (though not law) treats jury decision-making as a kind of holy secret. What are the facts? We have conducted a detailed interview with one of the jurors involved, and his evidence suggests that the DPP's self-justification is hopelessly off the mark.

The juror the magazine interviewed revealed that most of the jury rejected the charge of conspiracy to murder after one hour and spent the remainder of their two-day deliberation convincing the one holdout juror to make the acquittal unanimous. But he also said that the jury would have happily convicted everyone involved of a lesser charge had they been allowed: 'They were definitely guilty of something. All of them'. The *New Statesman* concluded:

> The jury appears to have been a reasonable cross-section of working-class and middle-class Londoners—a teacher, a young welder, two elderly office workers, a civil servant, secretaries and housewives. But the man we interviewed felt that he and his colleagues got little help from the Crown, although the prosecution lawyers in court did 'a very good case…with the little they had.'

The latter statement couldn't have hurt the career of the lead Crown counsel in Thorpe's prosecution, Peter Taylor QC, then on the cusp of judicial appointment.

The direct result of the *New Statesman*'s article was a test case on whether publishing details of jury deliberations was a contempt of court. After the Attorney-General conceded that the article 'is unexceptionable since the words published demonstrate that the jury approached its task in a sensible and responsible manner', England's then Lord Chief Justice John Widgery held that no crime was committed:

> Looking at this case as a whole, we have come to the conclusion that the article in the 'New Statesman' does not justify the title of contempt of court. That does not mean that we would not wish to see restrictions on the publication of such an article because we would.

That last sentence, in turn, prompted the UK Parliament to enact a new statute in 1981, the Contempt of Court Act, including section 8(1):

> It is a contempt of court to obtain, disclose or solicit any particulars of statements made, opinions expressed, arguments advanced or votes cast

by members of a jury in the course of their deliberations in any legal proceedings.

Although this provision was drafted to deal with journalists investigating jurors, a major issue in Young's appeal was whether and how it applied to courts investigating alleged juror misconduct.

'Three possibilities were canvassed' by the barristers before the Court of Appeal in Young's case:

> First, that the court could inquire into what happened at the hotel and what happened in the jury room thereafter. Second, that the court could inquire only into what occurred at the hotel. Third, that the court could not inquire at all into the jury's activities.

The first position was pressed by Young's lawyer, David Penry-Davey, who argued that 'public policy requires the court, in the interests of justice, to be able to look into any irregularities alleged to have occurred in the jury room'. The Court of Appeal rejected that argument:

> As a matter of principle, the object of the section is clearly to maintain the secrecy of the jury's deliberations in their retiring room. To give the court power, after verdict, to inquire into those deliberations, would force the door of the jury room wide open. If one dissentient juror or sharp-eared bailiff alleged irregularities in the jury room, the court would be pressed to inquire into the jury's deliberations. We are in no doubt that section 8(1) applies to the court as to everyone else.

The third position was supported by Michael Lawson for the prosecution:

> He argues that once the summing-up ends and the jury retire to consider their verdict or (as he puts it) once the jury is enclosed, section 8(1) applies and the veil must be drawn over the jury's activities. Counsel could not find any case relating to a jury's stay in an hotel. However, Mr Lawson submits

that the period of the jury's retirement from the moment the judge encloses them up to the return of their verdict, is indivisible.

As it happens, another case relating to a jury's stay in a hotel—the one discussed in *Chapter 1*, where the jury clearly deliberated overnight in the case of alleged fraud against the National Health Service—was about to be decided by a different trio of appeal judges. However, the Court of Appeal there did not need to look behind the jury's 'veil', because the jurors themselves admitted in open court what they intended to do at the hotel and the judge reluctantly acquiesced in their plan.

Dorian Lovell-Pank, the barrister acting as friend of the court for the arguments about secrecy, supported the defence's view, arguing that the Contempt of Court Act's purpose was to restrict the media, not the courts. But he also suggested a fall-back position that the Court of Appeal adopted:

> In our view, the whole object of sending a jury to an hotel is to give them a break, rest or respite from their deliberations. It would be absurd to suggest that when every juror is in a separate bedroom, whatever their thoughts, the jury could collectively be described as being 'in the course of their deliberations.'…In practice, judges tell juries that they should have a break from their deliberations until they return to their jury room next morning and should not deliberate at the hotel. The trial judge in the present case did just that. Mr. Lawson submits that whilst the judge can give guidance on this matter to the jury, his instruction is not a direction of law. Nevertheless, it underlines the reality of the situation, that a jury's stay in an hotel is in fact a hiatus between sessions in the jury room during which the jury as a whole is in the course of its deliberations.

This explains why the Court of Appeal ordered an inquiry into what happened at *The Old Ship* in Brighton, including the dinner, the breakfast, and everything in between, but not into anything that happened at the Crown Court in Hove.

Lovell-Pank's compromise pleased no-one other than the Court of Appeal. According to the media, Lawson had already told the court that in the defence's and Lovell-Pank's arguments 'lay the danger of the end of the jury system'. Young's solicitor, in a subsequent column in a professional magazine, wrote:

> When the Lord Chief Justice and two of his brethren were performing a delicate minuet around the veil of secrecy imposed by section 8, my mind wandered to the words of Dickens' street-wise bootblack, Sam Weller. 'It's over and can't be helped, and that's one consolation, as they always say in Turkey, ven they cuts the wrong man's head off.'

He called for urgent law reform to ensure that:

> ...the Court of Appeal is not to be allowed to stand by helplessly on the sidelines while defendants are convicted on the basis of false and irregular deliberations, whether those be founded on voodoo, black magic or merely a lack of comprehension of the proceedings.

On the other hand, Nicola Fuller's father, speaking to the media after Young's retrial:

> ...said he hoped the House of Lords would now overturn the Court of Appeal's decision to quash the first trial and order a retrial. 'It opened a legal minefield,' he said. The first jury's verdict was correct and it was wrong that jurors were questioned about their deliberations.

In an unfortunate spectacle, Michael Johnson's remarks were cut off by the head of police at the Old Bailey citing a rule forbidding interviews in the court precincts and sparking an 'altercation' after which Nicola's parents 'left to recover in the Victim Support suite'.

Events took an even less fortunate turn when the prosecution asked the Court of Appeal to certify an appeal to the House of Lords, an application that prosecutors must make 'within the period of fourteen days beginning with the date of the decision of the Court'. The court ordered Young's retrial on 24th October 1994, but its reasons weren't formally published until after that trial was over in mid-December. The prosecution applied for a certificate on 17th November 1994, presumably shortly after the court's reasons were supplied to the parties and, according to the Lord Chief Justice, around ten days too late:

> The position, in our view, is made quite clear by section 34, that the period of 14 days begins with the decision of the court, which we gave when we allowed the appeal and ordered a retrial. Subsection (2) of the section does allow the court to extend time, but only on the application of the defendant. The Crown have to make up their minds within 14 days or that is that. We are afraid we do not certify or grant leave.

Thus, the Johnsons, the prosecution, Professor Spencer and the wider community were denied an opportunity for the UK's top court to weigh in on the Ouija board case.

The Johnsons and Lawson would probably have been disappointed in any event. A decade later, in a different set of appeals, the House of Lords unanimously ruled that Penry-Davey was right and Lawson and the Court of Appeal were wrong when it came to the Contempt of Court Act:

> It is obvious that the court cannot release jurors, journalists or anyone else from the constraints of section 8(1). But it is going too far to suggest, as the Court of Appeal appears to have done in Young's case, that the trial court will be in contempt of itself if during the trial, having received allegations such as those made by the jurors in these cases, it investigates them and discloses the result of these investigations to counsel so that they may have an opportunity of making submissions about them to the court; or that the Court of Appeal in its turn, or persons acting under its direction, will be in contempt if the Court of Appeal decides that in the interests of justice the allegations must be investigated. The court must look to the common law for guidance as to the extent to which any such investigation is permissible.

This ruling that the Court of Appeal botched its application of the Contempt of Court Act was not enough to satisfy Spencer. He was equally unhappy with the 'common law' that the Lords said applied in its place.

Outside of the door

> If, however, the jurors had set up their ouija board in the jury-room at the court house, the Court of Appeal could have done nothing whatever about it: even though using a ouija board at court itself would surely have been even worse. That this situation is an odd one hardly needs saying. How can the law of a supposedly intelligent people produce a result like this?

Two hundred and ten years earlier, on 9th November 1785, when what is now London's oldest general daily newspaper was the city's youngest, *The Times* reported:

> A motion was made on Monday, in the Court of King's Bench, to set aside a verdict, and it was supported on an affidavit of two of the jurors, which stated that the jury not having been able to determine upon which verdict to bring in, there being six for finding for the plaintiff and six for the defendant, tossed up, when the plaintiff's friends won. It was acknowledged by counsel for the motion, that the verdict coincided with the opinion of the court, and Lord Mansfield asked was there any objection to the verdict? The counsel answered none; but that he relied upon a case reported in Sir John Strange...

Strange's report of the earlier case said that a jury verdict was set aside (despite also being, in the court's opinion, correct on the evidence) because the jury had reached it by drawing one of two pieces of paper marked with the letters P and D out of a hat. According to the *Times*, David Murray, the Earl of Mansfield, then near the end of his three decades as England's Lord Chief Justice, revealed a detail that Strange had left out of his report:

> that in that case the application was founded upon the application of the bailiff, who had locked in the jury, and saw them through the window — and not upon the application of jurors...

This detail was key because, as *The Times* noted: 'A legal correspondent observes that, had the affidavit on the above cause been admitted, the jury would have been liable to a writ of attainder' (that is, punishment for committing a felony). In short, the jurors reporting the coin toss were admitting committing a serious crime.

The *Times* formally reported on the case, named *Vezey v Delaval*, the following week:

> Lord Mansfield rejected the affidavits; and observed, it was highly probable other evidence could have been procured; that it would endanger every verdict, if the Jury was to give an account of what passed among themselves; they often change their opinions; that the defendant could not be injured, because if the verdict was against evidence, he might obtain a new trial on that ground.

Its report doesn't state what 'other evidence' Mansfield had in mind to prove that the jury 'tossed-up' (flipped a coin), but later reports of the same case have him saying that judges must learn about jurors' behaviour 'from some other source: such as from some person having seen the transaction through a window, or by some such other means'.

Twenty years later, England's Court of Common Pleas considered an affidavit from a jury foreman, Ralph Bridge, that:

> ...the jury not being agreed left the Court and were put into a room by themselves; that four were disposed to find a verdict for the Defendant, and eight, for the Plaintiffs; that one of those disposed to find for the Plaintiffs swore he would stay there till Saturday evening before he would find a verdict for the Defendant; that after some hours had elapsed in fruitless endeavours by Bridge to alter the opinion of those who inclined to a verdict for the Plaintiffs, it was proposed by several of the jury to draw lots, to which Bridge was induced to assent; that accordingly two pencils were produced of different lengths, that it was agreed that the longest pencil should be for the Plaintiffs and the shortest far the Defendant; that Bridge held the pencils and another juryman drew, and that the longest pencil being drawn,

Mansfield's Window

the jury went to the Chief Justice's lodgings and those of the jury who were for the Plaintiffs gave in the verdict for them.

England's then second most senior judge, Sir James Mansfield (no relation to Lord Mansfield), after conferring with other judges, said:

> We are all of opinion that the affidavit of a juryman cannot be received. It is singular indeed that almost the only evidence of which the case admits should be shut out but, considering the arts which might be used if a contrary rule were to prevail, we think it necessary to exclude such evidence. If it were understood to be the law that a juryman might set aside a verdict by such evidence, it might sometimes happen that a juryman, being a friend to one of the parties, and not being able to bring over his companions to his opinion, might propose a decision by lot, with a view afterwards to set wide the verdict by his own affidavit, if the decision should be against him.

In this case, there was a further affidavit from a non-juror, saying:

> ...that he followed the jury when they went to the room, and stood at the outside of the door, where he heard the jurymen arguing very violently and disagreeing with each other; that after some time he heard a proposal by some of the jury to draw lots whether the verdict should be given in favour of the Plaintiffs or the Defendant; that they were quiet for some time, and then came out of the room and went to the Chief Justice's lodgings, after which he was told by several of the jurymen how the verdict was, and the mode in which it had been decided.

This variation on Mansfield's window—listening through a solid door—was admissible, but wasn't enough to convince the Court of Common Pleas to overturn the jury's verdict.

The rule the Court of Appeal applied in the Ouija board case was much stricter than these earlier rulings, barring inquiries into deliberations no matter what was being investigated (high misdemeanours or not) and who was the source of the information (jurors or others). As an

Australian court later commented, the ruling seemingly shut Mansfield's window into the jury room altogether:

> It is not clear where this leaves Lord Mansfield's suggestion, about 200 years previously, that if an onlooker had noticed, through a window of the jury room, jurors using a ouija board, the verdict could have been impugned.

Of course, the Court of Appeal also took a narrow view of what counted as 'deliberations'. While this conveniently permitted an inquiry into the Ouija board incident, it was open to criticism from two sides. Using the Lord Chief Justice's own logic, 'If one dissentient juror or sharp-eared bailiff alleged irregularities' at the hotel, then 'the court would be pressed to inquire' into what happened there. On the other hand, such an inquiry could never go beyond the hotel, even if there were compelling reasons to look further.

Indeed, the available transcripts of the hearings in Young's appeal reveal that the Court of Appeal had some cause to investigate events inside the jury room itself:

> THE LORD CHIEF JUSTICE: At the moment we are minded to think that the contents of that letter should be investigated insofar as it relates to how the allegation of an irregularity arose and was communicated, but not in regard to anything which concerns the deliberations of the jury in the jury room. You will see that the third paragraph up from the bottom refers to some concern about that, but that is not a matter which we consider at this stage ought to be investigated.
>
> MR RUNDELL: Your Lordships' provisional view is that investigations of events should cease when the jury return to the jury room on the second day? Your Lordship has seen the handwritten complaint which goes on to deal with—
>
> THE LORD CHIEF JUSTICE: Yes, yes, I follow that. No, it should cease there at this stage certainly.

MR RUNDELL: Is your Lordship wanting to discover whether any reference was made to a ouija board?

THE LORD CHIEF JUSTICE: No. Absolutely not at this stage.

Clearly, Adrian's handwritten letter mentioned something that happened in the jury room, presumably on the morning after the hotel stay, the same morning the jury delivered its verdict. Neither the transcripts, the Court of Appeal's judgement nor the *News of the World* reveal what Adrian said. The possibilities range from the Ouija board's being briefly mentioned in passing (e.g. as a grim joke after the verdict was decided) to the entire jury's poring over the foreperson's notes of the séance before deciding on Young's guilt or innocence. Thanks to Lord Taylor's instructions, the Treasury Solicitor did not seek any information about Adrian's claim from the 12 jurors and the Court of Appeal made no findings about them.

But the absoluteness of the Court of Appeal's ban on probing deliberations in the jury room only lasted a decade. In 2004, the House of Lords held that the Contempt of Court Act was aimed at jurors speaking to everyone *except* the courts. Mansfield's window, wrongly covered in Young's case, was uncovered a decade later. But the question remained: exactly when and how could judges look through it?

The freedom to act irresponsibly

> The basic problem is that there is no such thing as 'the jury'. A jury is a collection of twelve individual people, press-ganged at random, and with nothing in common but the fact that they were the ones who could not get away.

Because of the general ban on investigating juror deliberations, people who have never been on a jury often draw on their own experiences of how people think and talk to imagine what happens inside a jury room.

Professor Spencer described such a theory of jurors in 'Seances, and the Secrecy of the Jury-Room':

> On juries, as in the world generally, there are likely to be four types of person: intelligent and sensible ones, unintelligent and sensible ones, intelligent but silly ones, and — most frightening of all — ones who are both unintelligent and silly. Whether the jury works well, adequately, badly or atrociously must always depend on which of these four groups predominates.

Like many things Spencer writes, his description is evocative and useful, but the catch is that different people will see quite different things in words like 'intelligent', 'unintelligent', 'sensible', 'silly', 'frightening' and so on. How, for instance, would the various members of Young's jury be classified by Spencer? Crucially, his word 'predominates' assumes a particular way that a 'collection of twelve individual people' will produce a joint or majority decision.

In the decade after Young's appeal, England's courts were repeatedly asked to contemplate how jurors should interact with each other. In October 2002, five days after eleven out of 12 jurors found a man guilty of arranging a fire for insurance purposes, a juror wrote to a letter to the court. In summary, she alleged:

> (a) Despite the usher's warning not to make racist remarks, disparaging remarks were made throughout the trial by some members of the jury about the defendant's appearance, his accent, his poor English, his mannerisms, and his business integrity...
>
> (b) Some members of the jury appeared to have reached a decision at the outset of the trial and did not change their minds.
>
> (c) During the trial, newspapers dealing with the trial were brought into the jury retiring room by jurors and shown around.

(d) At least three jurors had mobile phones and two of them used them to contact outsiders during the trial and to tell them about the progress of the trial.

(e) A juror fell asleep during the evidence.

(f) A juror was deaf and could not hear all the evidence.

(g) Other members of the jury adopted a bullying attitude.

Citing both *Young* and the common law, the Court of Appeal held that it must ignore everything in this list and refrain from further inquiries. Spencer's response, in an article on the new case, was to double down on his criticism of juror secrecy:

> If juries are composed of twelve people chosen from the electoral roll at random, it is inevitable that they will sometimes be dominated by people who are racists, or irresponsible and silly, and our legal system is gravely deficient if it fails to guard against the obvious danger.

Again, the worth of this criticism turns on the meaning you give to its various terms, such as 'racists' and 'irresponsible' and 'dominated', which could either refer to the extremes of juror misbehaviour or just the usual foibles of 12 random people. The same problem arose in two further cases about jury letters that finally reached the House of Lords in 2004, a decade after the Ouija board case.

One letter raised a more specific complaint of racism, where 'some of the jury' came to suspect that a defendant was using an interpreter unnecessarily and 'shouted down' the letter writer when she cited a trial judge's direction telling them the issue was irrelevant. She added that 'I was the only juror with an insight into the defendant's culture'. The other letter read:

> There was an overall feeling that most of the people were looking for a quick verdict ie they did not want to be there until the end of the week or

longer. One of the Jurors had made references to other people that had been in the Press recently and when challenged about this, gave their verdict and then refused to participate anymore, doodling and reading a paper. There was talk of trying to reach a verdict by the tossing of a coin, this was quickly given short shrift.

The most worrying was that although many thought it could be one defendant or another they would give the guilty verdict to both, because as many of them said this would teach them a lesson, things in this life were not fair and sometimes innocent people would have to pay the price. Also as the defendants were young, the sentence would not be too severe.

When I raised objections to this, and said we must then look at whether it was one or the other, they maintained their guilty stance, and said that we could be here for another week. I said better that, than convict an innocent man, but then it developed into bedlam, and the majority guilty verdict was agreed.

After a majority of the House of Lords rejected both appeals, Spencer responded with a third article entitled 'Juries: The Freedom to Act Irresponsibly'.

But, for the House of Lords majority, these tales of jury disorder were a feature of the system, not a bug:

> Jurors are drawn from all walks of life. Many of them will be unaccustomed to discussing an issue in such company in a structured way. Their deliberations may be stormy requiring the reconciliation of strongly held views.

An example is the revelation that, in one case before the House of Lords, one or more jurors mooted tossing a coin to resolve the deadlock but the idea was 'given short shrift'. Even the dissenting Lord, who agreed with Spencer on the dangers of jury confidentiality, held that such a tentative discussion 'could not possibly support a ground of appeal'.

One thing that makes such problems easier to accept today is that the length of modern trials and deliberations gives the jurors plenty of time to seek help from the trial judge if their discussions go awry. In one of the cases before the Lords, the jury wanted to ask the interpreter 'In your experience as a Court interpreter would it be typical for a man of the defendant's background to require your services, despite living in this country as long as he has?' After consulting with counsel, the trial judge told the jury:

> What would you think if your friend or relation was denied an interpreter on the basis, well, they can understand a bit of Spanish; why should they have an interpreter? Look at it that way; and this was the sort of case where you are entitled to understand not only most or some of what is said in your trial, but every single word. So that in those circumstances you should draw no adverse inferences from the defendant exercising his right to have an interpreter.

In the other case before the Lords, there was an incident just as the verdict was delivered:

> The jury retired for four hours and forty-six minutes prior to being given the majority direction. After another two hours they returned to give their verdicts. Initially they found Ashley Rollock not guilty whereupon there was a disturbance amongst them and the learned judge asked them to retire to again discuss their verdicts. The jury returned within four minutes and found both defendants guilty by a majority of 10:2.

Again, all the Lords were untroubled by these events: 'It is not unusual for disagreements about the length of discussions to arise'.

But not all jury incidents are so easy to dismiss. In his note on the House of Lords decision, Spencer eloquently set out the two hardest scenarios for the common law rule:

> But how this will help if all the jurors are involved in the irregularity has yet to be explained; and similarly, how will it prevent miscarriages of justice where those who are not involved in the irregularity are too timid to complain at the time?

The latter, of course, was the situation in Young's trial. As Adrian told the *News of the World*:

> I thought I should have said something at the time, but because of my age I wasn't taken seriously. They felt I hadn't had much experience in life.

The majority of the Lords thought the answer was to actively encourage such complaints during the trial:

> To this end the jury must be told of their right and duty both individually or collectively to inform the court clerk or the judge in writing if they believe that anything untoward or improper has come to their notice. The judge can then deal with the matter in an appropriate way. He already has to deal with such matters as improper approaches to the jury, an unexpected recognition of or knowledge of a defendant or a witness and personal difficulties of jurors and has a power, within limits, to discharge individual jurors. He may of course, if necessary, discharge the whole jury and start again.

The shadow of the Ouija board case also loomed large over Spencer's other, less tractable quandary, concerning the possibility of misconduct by 'all the jurors'.

An embarrassing situation

> Last year, for example, the Court of Appeal also heard an appeal from a conviction in a murder case where one of the defendants complained that a woman juror had spent her time in the jury-box falling in love with one of the barristers with whom she tried to make a date after the court had risen.

On 1st July 1994, while Young's jurors were being interviewed by a superintendent, the Court of Appeal decided the case mentioned by Professor Spencer. It concerned a murder at Cambridge's Christ's Pieces, which the prosecution said was the result of a murky dispute between four people over money. The jury unanimously convicted one of the accused, unanimously acquitted a second and, after further deliberation, convicted the third by majority. Between the second and third verdicts, a juror handed a court clerk a sealed envelope addressed to the acquitted defendant's barrister. The envelope contained a handwritten letter, which the trial judge read aloud in the presence of all three counsel:

Dear Mr Hubbard,

I hope that you won't think me impertinent for writing. I mean no disrespect to you. I realise that it is highly irregular but I have a question I would like to ask. Would it be at all possible for you to consider an invitation for a drink with me either before leaving Norwich or maybe if you return some time in the future? Of course I do not wish to place you in an embarrassing situation and will quite understand if you should decline. But just in case there is a slight possibility of you accepting... I hope that I haven't offended you. It has taken a lot of courage writing this letter and I must admit to being somewhat embarrassed.

The letter included the juror's phone number and her name.

Spencer mentions this example to illustrate how 'bizarre and irresponsible behaviour by jurors... certainly does happen, both in the jury-room and out of it'. But, again, different people will view these events—in whichever room they occur—in different ways. Is the mere fact of becoming sexually or otherwise attracted to a barrister (or, as the professor quaintly describes it, 'falling in love') during a trial either 'bizarre' or 'irresponsible'? Or is it the juror's decision to write and supply the letter during the trial that merits that description? Not all would agree that the former is especially strange or blameworthy, though much depends on context (and, perhaps, upon the barrister, in this instance Michael Hubbard QC, renowned for his 'powerful voice' and later famous for defending a notorious killer's girlfriend, Maxine Carr). As for the latter, such criticisms are fairer, but there are also other, less judgemental, ways to label the juror's entreaty to Hubbard: naïve, emotional, silly or, to use the juror's own description, somewhat embarrassing. A further way of looking at the case is that it is a rare instance of a juror's emotional life during a trial, one that is unlikely to be unique, being publicly revealed.

There is nothing especially rare about jurors acting in ways that some would label bizarre, irresponsible or embarrassing. In the same six-month period in 1994 when Young's appeal was being heard, England's Court of Appeal ruled on arguments about a juror who complained repeatedly about a conflicting social engagement, one who giggled at the defendant, another (the foreman) who grimaced at the accused, one whose husband attended the courtroom when the jury were sent out, another whose objections to 'obscene language' caused the dismissal of her panel, a further set who mingled with a new jury panel after theirs was dismissed, a note from the foreperson claiming that other jurors had a 'closed mind', a claim that a juror knew the defendant, and a foreman who dozed through parts of the trial. What is telling, though, is that the Court of Appeal only allowed appeals in two of those cases: the Ouija board case and the case (discussed in *Chapter 1*) where the jurors clearly deliberated overnight at their Birmingham hotel. This wasn't because the courts either chose not to know what happened in the remaining cases or endorsed how the jurors behaved, but rather because the response of courts to such claims always depends heavily on the particular circumstances.

An example is the Court of Appeal's response in the case where the juror asked a barrister on a date. In its judgement, the court said that, had the letter to Hubbard emerged and the defendant raised an issue with it before the jury started deliberating, 'a judge would probably discharge the juror and continue the trial with 11 jurors so as to avoid any appearance of bias'. But what actually happened was that the letter emerged mid-deliberations and none of the trial barristers thought it mattered; indeed, the barrister whose client was still awaiting a verdict simply said: 'I don't think this affects my client'. So, when that same defendant later raised the letter as a ground to appeal against his conviction, the Court of Appeal endorsed his barrister's 'instinctive and immediate reaction'. It was, the judges said, 'most unlikely that this juror communicated her liking for leading counsel for Stafford to other jurors, and still less likely that had she done so the other jurors would have allowed their judgements to be swayed by that disclosure'. There are plenty of counter-factuals—the letter being directed to the Crown's barrister, the precise terms of the juror's letter, the circumstances in which it was handed over, the response of the barristers, perhaps even the juror being the foreperson—where the outcome could well have been a new trial.

The Ouija board incident could never have been dealt with by simply dismissing those involved in the séance, because a murder trial cannot continue with only eight jurors. Penry-Davey's view on the hypothetical of a mid-trial revelation was that 'if the events in the hotel had come to light before delivery of the verdict, the only proper course would have been to discharge the jury'. That is very likely correct, but the outcome could still have been affected by particular circumstances: precisely when the evidence emerged, how it emerged, what stance each barrister took and what the jurors involved said about the incident. For example, had the bailiffs brought the breakfast table conversation to the trial judge's attention that morning (during the two remaining hours that the jury formally deliberated) and the foreman immediately explained (and Penry-Davey immediately accepted) that the incident was a mere game, then the trial judge may well have opted to continue the trial, just as happened when the juror's letter to Hubbard was revealed. And, had events played out in that way, then the Court of Appeal might likewise have deferred to the trial participants' immediate instincts. Because the incident didn't emerge in this way, we will never know.

Horror stories

> If such cases are statistically rare, their rarity is no consolation to the hapless defendant in the case, whom the jurors' vagaries, in a murder case, may have landed life imprisonment.

In 2004, the House of Lords considered a very different Ouija board hypothetical, closely resembling the one Spencer raised in 'Seances and the Secrecy of the Jury-Room' nine years earlier. Lord Johan Steyn described it like this:

> For example, adapting the facts of *R v Young*, it is accepted by counsel for the Director of Public Prosecutions, that if the jury brought an ouija board into the jury room and determined the issue by consulting it, the exclusionary rule would not apply. Evidence may then be led about what actually happened. It would, of course, be absurd not to allow such evidence to be led. On the other hand, counsel for the Director of Public Prosecutions felt constrained to argue that, if the foreman of a jury took a coin out of his pocket in the jury room, the evidence about the tossing of a coin in the jury room to obtain a verdict, was inadmissible. Such absurd distinctions do not reflect well on our jurisprudence.

Steyn's adaptation of 'the facts of *R v Young*' involves at least four alterations to the actual events in the Ouija board case: a real Ouija board (rather than paper and a glass), its use inside the jury room (rather than a hotel room), its use by all 12 jurors (rather than only four of them) and its use to 'determine... the issue', rather than the scenario of specious external 'influence' feared by the Court of Appeal a decade earlier.

None of the changes is minor. The use of an actual board suggests premeditation and seriousness rather than spontaneity and jocularity, and involves the use of a much more unusual item than a glass, paper or coin. The other three factors all point unequivocally to a plan to use the séance to inform the jury's deliberations. Indeed, despite Steyn's claim about 'absurd distinctions', there is a quite important difference between using a Ouija board and tossing a coin. Ouija boards take the form (and are accepted by some to capture the reality) of actual communication about events. The Ouija board jurors asked specific questions and obtained specific answers about key factual disputes in the trial. By contrast, except perhaps for a vague belief in fate, no-one sees a single coin toss as a method of uncovering an empirical truth; rather, it is used as a simple, albeit completely arbitrary, way of overcoming an impasse in decision-making. So, while there are plenty of examples in the law reports of (plausible) claims about jurors tossing coins and drawing lots and the like, all of them are from the era where trial judges used to force indecisive juries to reach a verdict, for example confining them and even starving them until they did so. Modern examples of such arbitrary decision-making processes are non-existent.

There has only ever been one reported case about jurors using a Ouija board, and it was completely different to the scenario discussed by Steyn. Nevertheless, Lord David Hope responded to the Ouija board hypothetical by endorsing a new exception to the common law rule on jury secrecy:

> An allegation that the jury as a whole declined to deliberate at all, but decided the case by other means such as drawing lots or by the toss of a coin, can be placed into a different category. Conduct of that kind, were it ever to occur, would amount to a complete repudiation by the jury of their only function which, as the juror's oath puts it, is to give a true verdict according to the evidence. A trial which results in a verdict by lot or the toss of a coin, or was reached by consulting an ouija board in the jury room, is not a trial at all. If that is what happened, the jurors have no need to be protected as the verdict was not reached by deliberation — that is, by discussing and debating the issues in the case and arriving at a decision collectively in the light of that discussion. The law would be unduly hampered if the court were to be unable to intervene in such a case and order a new trial.

As Hope made clear, 'that is not the situation which is before us in these appeals'. Nor has such an allegation been made since the coin tossing and lot drawing cases of Mansfield's era.

Of course, the absence of evidence is not evidence of absence. Because of jury secrecy, we have no way of knowing if other juries have used Ouija boards, including inside the jury room. Lord Hope's exception for misconduct by the jury 'as a whole' is unlikely to change that situation, because, by definition, it depends on reporting by someone who participated in extreme misconduct. Spencer's view is that the mere possibility of such an event occurring without detection merits drastic solutions, such as recording all jury deliberations or changing the entire jury system. But the case for such steps rests on assumptions or guesswork about how likely it is that jurors will misbehave in such extreme ways.

That is where Spencer's 'dossier' comes in. In 2013, he told YouTube:

The Ouija Board Jurors

Most people who are called for jury service are serious, or at any rate enough of them are serious enough to see that the serious ones predominate. But, as the horror stories I have just given you show, this is by no means always so and sometimes irresponsible people, or very ill-informed people, or very timorous people, predominate.

But, with the arguable exception of the Ouija board case, the examples of juror misconduct he cites don't involve any such domination or significant irresponsibility. For example, in the case of the two drunken jurors, five others left the birthday lunch in question after trying to persuade the two to stop drinking. In the other case, where a juror texted her fiancé in the public gallery, the remaining jurors denied hearing anything untoward and an examination of the juror's phone showed that the pair exchanged innocuous information (e.g. about the timing of lunch). The Court of Appeal ordered a new trial because of 'apprehended bias', that is, that it would be reasonable for an onlooker to fear that more significant information was exchanged at some other point.

Steyn, alone in the House of Lords in 2004, was convinced by Spencer's earlier observation that:

> The fact that many allegations of this sort are false cannot justify ignoring all of them because, as Young painfully reminds us, some of them regrettably are true.

True the facts of the Ouija board case were, but whether they amount to a 'horror story' is much less clear, depending (amongst other things) on how you define 'horror'.

The absurdities of life

> When such things do happen, it is obviously vital to be able to do something about them, whether the scene of the jurors' irresponsible behaviour was the hotel, the court-room, or the jury-room itself.

Professor Spencer is rightly feted for 'his often highly entertaining articulation of the most complex scenarios'. He is indeed a skilled summariser, to considerable educational and entertaining effect. But, as an imprecise description of the Ouija board case by one of his Cambridge colleagues attests, his concise style can sometimes give his readers and listeners the wrong impression of complex cases:

> John certainly sees the absurdities of life—the reliance by a jury on a Ouija board to find out who done it being one—but unlike [fictional curmudgeon] Victor Meldrew, John has a wicked sense of humour, and a capacity to reduce a rapt audience to fits of laughter as he tells one of his (risqué) jokes.

Notably, the Professor's colleague ignores Spencer's own distinction between 'the jury' and jurors. But, then again, so does Spencer himself on occasions, for example, the title 'Seances and the Secrecy of the Jury-Room', summarising a case that involved neither the jury room nor two-thirds of the jury.

Spencer's use of humour, while gifted, entertaining and engaging, also conceals what I believe is the key to understanding the case. While Young's first trial judge made no comment when he sentenced the broker to two life sentences, his second trial judge spelt out how heavily the trial would have weighed on everyone involved:

> The jury has convicted you of terrible and horrible offences. Two human beings were shot by you quite brutally. The circumstances of the deaths of both of them are truly horrifying. The precise circumstances of Nicola Fuller's death will stay in everybody's minds for years to come.

Those last words were prophetic. Three years later, one of the jurors in Young's second trial told English television viewers his account of the case, which was a world away from 'the absurdities of life':

> First of all they tell you he was going to be…prosecuted for murder—and then they describe what actually happened and it…sort of…you go cold. You know, even though you're physically warm, your legs go cold. It's as if your blood doesn't want to go near your skin.

'David' narrates the real 'horror story' that lies within the Ouija board case.

CHAPTER 6

The Horrid Part

The previous jury — A little levity — Your worst nightmare — Empty shells — Channelling the victim — Each one alone — The choice

Around the time that Adrian's jury was hearing evidence against Stephen Young, the Dean of Warwick University's Law School, Professor Mike McConville, organized a conference for victims and survivors of crime. To his surprise, amongst the hundreds of victims who responded to his call for participants were several jurors:

> They recounted some of their experiences in graphic detail, as if it were yesterday, even if the trial had been years before. In court they were sworn to secrecy, so they felt they could not talk to anybody about what they had seen. One of the cases was the brutal killing of a child where the juror had been required to look at photographic evidence that was very gruesome.

McConville was quoted in a *Sunday Times* article previewing a documentary in the BBC's *Modern Times* series broadcast in England in mid-April 1997. The documentary featured interviews with several anonymous jurors.

One sat in the 1993 trial of Paul Esslemont, who was charged with killing a three-year-old in Coventry. Sixteen-year-old Esslemont was a friend of the toddler's older brother and helped the child's mother after she found the family dog shaking in fright. He even called the police and later guided a police officer during the search that eventually located the toddler's body. The prosecution's case at the mid-1993 trial was that

Esslemont strangled the toddler with the boy's t-shirt and then beat him to death with his golf club. Based on blood on the teen's trainers and golf club, the jury found him guilty of manslaughter by a 10:2 majority. During Young's first trial in March 1994, Lord Chief Justice Taylor, in his judgement for the Court of Appeal, upheld Esslemont's conviction.

Ann, the juror interviewed by *Modern Times*, revealed that she visited the scene of the toddler's death shortly after the trial:

> I thought if I could go to the place where it happened it would help me to come to terms with it. There was a stream, some waste ground and a children's playground. I sat on the swings. Being at the scene of the crime was cathartic. It helped me work through some of the grief.

The BBC documentary also featured jurors from two much higher profile cases: the 1981 trial of the Yorkshire Ripper, and one of the trials following the Strangeways prison riot of 1990. The final case *Modern Times* featured was the Fuller case, specifically Young's retrial at the Old Bailey in November and December 1994, which the Court of Appeal ordered because of the Ouija board incident.

'David', a member of the new jury, described his thoughts on first seeing Young at the dock:

> You know I was expecting an ogre to walk in and it was quite scary to think that this ordinary looking chap had committed murder or could commit murder at that point.

Although Young's alleged crime—the shooting of two adults—was arguably the least horrific of the four covered in the documentary, David spent part of his interview, some two years after the trial, on the verge of tears. His distress was due to a particular piece of evidence introduced at both of Young's trials.

Three weeks after the Fullers' deaths, an Operation Arrowhead officer had pressed the 'redial' button on the phone handset that had been found lying next to Nicola Fuller. The police officer's goal was simply to find out who the couple might have spoken to that morning or the night before. He was surprised to discover that the last call on her handset was to 999, the United Kingdom emergency number. The Wadhurst police hadn't received any calls on the morning the Fullers died.

This chapter explores the evidence that flowed from the officer's chance discovery. While that evidence ended up playing only a minor role in the prosecution case, it prompted the dismissal of one jury panel and, as David outlined, had a profound effect on another. Although speculative, the evidence provides a possible reason as to why some jurors used a makeshift Ouija board in Young's first trial and why several cried as they did so.

The previous jury

> This was a recorded phone message. Somebody had been shot and they picked up the phone and dialled 999 and, because they were shot in the head, they couldn't talk properly. So, the whole tape was actually described to us first, so we were well aware of what was going on.

The first jurors empanelled to try Stephen Young, seven women and five men, were sworn in at Hove Crown Court on Monday 21st February 1994. The next morning, during Michael Lawson's opening speech, a 'hushed court' listened to a tape of Nicola Fuller's 999 call.

In this case of many recorded phone calls, this one was a routine recording of incoming calls made by a British Telecom call centre, specifically one that referred 999 callers in Sussex to the appropriate emergency service. The first 17 seconds of the tape included Nicola's final 'pitiful squeals' as her killer placed a duvet over her head, as well as a muffled bang and the sound of the phone handset falling to the floor. The following day, with Lawson's opening speech only half done, a juror sent a note to the trial judge asking to be excused from the trial because the evidence was 'too distressing'.

The Fuller case would have been a sharp change of pace and tone for Mr Justice Christopher French. Appointed as a High Court judge 15 years earlier, he initially served on the Family Division before a career on the Queen's Bench. He presided over trials ranging from a thalidomide case to a landmark action over local council loans (which ultimately gave birth to the modern law of restitution) and the prosecution of IRA terrorist John McComb. In the year before Young's trial, he heard 'one of the longest, most complicated and most expensive civil actions ever heard before a British court' — an action over a cluster of young cancer deaths near Sellafield nuclear power station — and was widely praised for his detailed judgement rejecting the theory that the children's deaths were caused by their fathers' work at the plant. Presiding over a double murder trial in Hove Crown Court just four months later, French responded to the juror's request to be excused by discharging the whole jury. The new panel he swore in included Adrian and the four who later gathered in a hotel room to use a makeshift Ouija board.

The discharge of entire jury panels is not unusual. Indeed, in Paul Esslemont's murder trial nine months earlier, the first jury was discharged several days into the case because one of them fell asleep. While judges have the options of refusing to excuse (or dismiss) a juror or persevering with a slightly reduced jury, they will often opt to start afresh if an incident occurs early enough in the trial. Trial judges must balance two costs: the expense of stopping a partly completed trial and the risk of the trial's outcome being overturned on appeal due to a problem with the jury panel. This calculus favours discharging the panel for early incidents but persevering for later ones. It also means that jurors face increasing pressure to stay on in their role as the trial continues, or if an earlier trial failed.

In Esslemont's trial, the trial judge made this pressure explicit, by telling the new jury (including 'Ann') that the sleeping juror had cost the system around five thousand pounds:

> There is no mystery. We had an embarrassing situation when one of the jurors fell asleep. It was quite remarkable but there it is. I tell you this for two reasons, I don't want you speculating that something strange happened and because it is vitally important that you feel able to concentrate. If

anybody starts to feel sleepy we will have a 10-minute break, and that is much better than the terrible situation we had.

French simply told Young's new jury: 'Unhappily one of the previous jury having heard the distressing nature of the case felt that he or she could no longer continue'.

The Fuller case preceded a sudden decline in French's career. He was widely-known for his keen horse-riding and lengthy, fast-paced walks with his five terriers. Before the Sellafield trial, the media reported that he 'used to say that when it comes to the heart, it has to be exercise that makes you puff. And he likes a challenge: he will rise to it'. But, a year after Young's trial, the 70-year-old underwent open heart surgery. He returned to the bench in 1996 in seeming good health, presiding over a defamation trial involving Imran Kahn and Ian Botham. One reporter wrote:

> There is only one sex symbol in the courtroom and he is not a cricketer. French has won female spectators over with wit, a roguish smile and a head boyish amusement at the nature of the proceedings...a former Captain in the Coldstream Guards, has drawn ooohs, giggles and the occasional downright phwooargh.

However, later that year, he heard another major defamation matter, a month-long civil jury trial hearing a complaint by former Irish Taoiseach Albert Reynolds against *The Times*. The case went on to be another landmark, with the House of Lords using it to develop the defamation defence of qualified privilege. However, before the Lords ruled on the law, the Court of Appeal dealt with French's conduct, specifically his 170-page direction to the jury, delivered over the course of week because of the illness of some jurors and debates over legal issues.

The court didn't mince words. Peter Taylor's successor, Lord Chief Justice Tom Bingham, wrote:

> The summing-up was indeed long, and the judge did little to relate the evidence to the specific issues. It cannot have been an easy direction to

assimilate. We have considerable sympathy with the jury in their task of seeking to analyse large tracts of undigested material. But defects of form or presentation would not entitle Mr Reynolds to the relief he seeks unless the misdirections complained of, singly or cumulatively, lead us to the opinion that 'some substantial wrong or miscarriage has been thereby occasioned'…With very great regret, because we are mindful of the consequences, we conclude that the misdirections which we have identified above were, cumulatively, such as to have that effect.

Others were blunter. A legal commentator told *The Times* that French 'was still recovering from the operation and did not have the concentration or powers of recall that he once had. No-one was surprised when he retired a few months later.' Sir Christopher died six years later, after which legal commentator Joshua Rozenberg wrote:

His death leaves me to write what I wish about him: the ultimate defence to a claim for libel is that the claimant is no longer alive. However, all I shall say is that there needs to be a better way of ensuring that judges whose powers are in decline through age or illness do not carry on sitting.

A little levity

> You heard the sound of the tape with the phone ringing. You heard the operator on the emergency phone number say 'This is an emergency can I help you?' and the woman who had been shot was just garbling and she was saying 'Help I've been shot.'

Stephen Young's November retrial was put in a safe pair of hands. Mr Justice John Blofeld, aged 62, was the presiding member for the South Eastern Circuit and a veteran of many complex criminal trials. His shared surname with the most infamous James Bond villain is no coincidence. Henry Blofeld, the judge's cricket commentator brother, claimed that Ian Fleming named Ernst Blofeld after their father Thomas, who was in the author's year at Eton. But the judge's son Tom's theory is that Fleming took the 'foreign-sounding appendages' of his villains, including the cat-stroking leader of SPECTRE, from the prefect list of his nephew Nichol Fleming's school. That theory gains significant support from the fact that a fellow student of John Blofeld's that year shared his surname with Fleming's *The Man With the Golden Gun*. In 2015, Sunningdale Preparatory School's principal told *The Mail on Sunday*: 'What I have always been told is that [Peter] Scaramanga and [John] Blofeld were not terribly nice to [Nichol] Fleming so Ian Fleming used them as the baddies in the books'. The judge, for his part, gave the *Mail* a less than full denial: 'Whether I was at school with a boy called Fleming, or whether I was nasty to a boy called Fleming, I have absolutely no idea'.

Blofeld told Young's Old Bailey jury:

> The case has attracted a great deal of publicity. If any of you consider that because of that publicity you might not be able to try the case impartially, please say now.

The judge's caution about 'publicity' doubtless drew on his own recent experiences. In 1992, he presided over the trial of two sisters for the stabbing murder of Alison Shaughnessy, which was accompanied by sensationalist press coverage of a 'Judas kiss' between one of the sisters and the victim's husband. Despite Blofeld's repeated warnings to the jury to disregard the reports, the Court of Appeal overturned the conviction the following year and declined to order a retrial, citing the 'risk of prejudice' created by the media's repeated publication of a still from the victim and defendant's wedding video. A few months before Young's retrial, Blofeld was prominently named in the press with two other judges for alleged collusion and bias in the trial and appeal of an accused drug-trafficker. The press gave little attention to the judges' complete denials or the speedy dropping of the allegations.

But Blofeld's concerns went beyond contamination by the press. He also told the jury of the 'holiday camp atmosphere' of the previous jury deliberations, a phrase he must have drawn from the *News of the World* report seven months earlier. The juxtaposition of Adrian's description and the prosecution evidence would have been jarring to jurors such as David:

> To actually deal with a murder case and to go through all the emotions that go with that murder case because you can't sit there and not get involved. It's too much…

But the occasional role of levity even in the most serious trials was publicly acknowledged a year earlier by the trial judge at the trial of Paul Esslemont:

> This is without doubt a very serious case. No-one can pretend otherwise. No-one who stops and thinks about it could think otherwise. There have been odd moments during the course of the case when there has been a little humour, a little levity. It must be very hard for the parents of the little boy, if they are present; for the parents of the defendant and the rest of the family to understand how that can come about when we are considering such an important matter, but, members of the jury, to consider matters of this kind over a period of what is now weeks without there being such moments becomes intolerable and it is natural, it is proper that there will be such moments. But no-one should think for one moment that any of that in any way detracts from the seriousness of the task that you are going to have to perform.

This rare discussion of the role of gallows humour in criminal trials, including amongst jurors, explains how it can make the intolerable bearable. By contrast, Blofeld's warning left no doubt that such emotional relief was to play no part in Young's retrial, instead cautioning the jury that such behaviour could prompt an agonising third trial.

On *Modern Times*, David told of his efforts to avoid serving as a juror before he was empanelled:

> Jury service is something that you think happens to other people and when it happens to you, you don't want to do it. How can I get out of this? That was my first thought. I don't need to do the… I haven't got time to do this.

I don't want to go this. So, I just filled it in and thought well there's enough reasons there why I don't have to do it and they were going to send back the letter saying you don't have to do it, but it actually said you're going to go.

However, none of the jury of three women and nine men, including David, took up the trial judge's offer to leave by claiming partiality (though one was replaced due to family obligations).

Your worst nightmare

> We knew she was saying that because we knew at that point she'd been shot and we were expecting that kind of statement. But the woman at the other end was saying: 'Look, if there's a problem, can you get your mummy?'

In summing up, Blofeld told the jury:

We know that at 8.43.34 the 999 call starts and the horrid part of this case is the thought of Mrs Nicola Fuller desperately injured, crawling or staggering from the stairs to her bedroom in order to try and get help. She gets through. She does not make herself heard.

When Nicola spoke to the British Telecom operator, she had a shoulder wound from one bullet, a splintered skull at her hairline from a second and, worst of all, a shattered eye, damaged tongue and splintered jaw after a third passed through her cheek.

'David' described his response to listening to the tape this way:

It was like your worst nightmare. I've watched American police programmes and they've got murder every 15 seconds and you see pools of blood on the ground and chalk lines drawn where bodies were and bullets picked up and you see people screaming and shouting. That's nothing compared to the sound of this tape. Nothing. You cannot believe the shock that runs through you. You cannot believe the fear that you feel when you know that this is what happens.

For Nicola's relatives, the tape exponentially increased their grief. While Nicola's parents didn't listen to it, her sister did. Michael Johnson told the media:

> Michelle, my other daughter, heard the tape of Nicola who cried, 'Police, police' and then screamed before a shot was heard, yet the operator assumed it was the gurglings of a two-year-old. The police station was 200 yards away and the killer could have been caught red-handed and my daughter might have lived.

The latter suggestion is unlikely, not only because Nicola had already been shot three times by then, but also because her killer shot her a fourth time a short way into the phone call. But the claim that 'the killer could have been caught red-handed' gains support from the criminal's seeming obliviousness to what was happening on the phone. Had the police come to Blackmans Cottage promptly (without tipping-off the killer of their impending arrival), then they would almost certainly have caught the murderer red-handed carrying incriminating items such as cash, bullet casings or a weapon, either confirming Young's guilt or exonerating him.

After Young was convicted, Michael called for such 'life-or-death decisions' to be taken out of the hand of telephone operators. British Telecom responded that it had 'held an immediate refresher course at the operator centre' and that 'this issue will now be included in regular training', while defending the operator's efforts to establish whether the caller was a child. A week later, Barbara Johnson told the media that the couple had met with British Telecom:

> We wanted to know why they didn't put the call through to the police. We were treated with disdain and they wanted to get us out of the premises as soon as possible. I have had other operators ringing me up to say they are trained to put calls like this through to the police, and they are horrified that this call didn't get through.

Her husband added:

> We would like them to explain in public, exactly what happened and why it happened. Also, we have never had any apology from them. It's just not good enough.

But British Telecom would only say:

> BT expresses its sympathy towards Mr and Mrs Johnson over the loss of their daughter. However, internal disciplinary procedures are a matter for BT only. We are constantly reviewing our procedures for different types of 999 calls, all of which have been agreed by the Home Office and emergency authorities.

There are at least three likely reasons why the Johnsons' complaints went nowhere.

First, the Johnsons said that they wanted the operator who took Nicola's call sacked. While their anger is understandable, their stance lacks empathy with the operator's own predicament (and, indeed, the burdens placed on all such operators). According to the media:

> BT managers said that the operator had been left deeply shocked. She had been on sick leave for months and the company had to look after her. An internal disciplinary inquiry was under way into what went wrong but the results would remain confidential.

Second, the Johnsons threatened a civil suit:

> I have no alternative but to sue. Their attitude was that the operator had made a mistake but that was the end of it. They refused to identify the operator and said that their disciplinary procedures were none of my concern. Although they admitted the error, they told me that they would continue operating the same system of filtering emergency calls which had been agreed with Oftel and the Home Office. It is appalling and if this is the case the public has a right to know.

The Ouija Board Jurors

A civil complaint would probably have failed. Two decades later, a majority of the United Kingdom Supreme Court held that British emergency services cannot be sued in negligence for failing to respond to a 999 call, unless the operator promised to respond and the caller relied on that. The Johnsons' only option would have been to bring a claim (against the United Kingdom, rather than British Telecom) in the European Court of Human Rights.

The couple's legal brinkmanship allowed British Telecom to withdraw from the discussion:

> Considering Mr Johnson's statement that he is to sue the company, we have no further comment to make. The matter is now in the hands of our solicitors.

The litigation never commenced. The likely explanation is the third reason why the complaint against BT went nowhere. Within days of the Johnsons going to the press, the *News of the World* broke the story that Young's jurors had consulted a Ouija board.

Empty shells

> The journey home on the train was very quiet. Very quiet. It just… I didn't read. I didn't… I didn't say… I didn't think but just one thought was on my mind and you couldn't think of anything else. Nothing was allowed in, you know, it was… just… you went over and over and over again…

David's halting account sounds like that of a victim of crime:

> It was quite a cold winter's day anyway and I got indoors and straight in the shower. I felt dirty. I wanted to get washed more so than normal. I just wanted to get clean and I kept saying to my wife: 'Why isn't the heating on?' I said 'Turn the heating up' and I felt cold. I kept shivering and she said it's too hot in here in the first place. I said… so I went and got another

cardigan, put thicker socks on and she kept talking to me and I kept saying 'Pardon?' I want…I knew there were words going on in the room, but I didn't hear what words she said and I actually had to stop and say 'Right now, talk, I'm now ready to listen'. It was crazy and I couldn't hear what she was saying. Do I just…I knew that today had been too much. That day had been too much for me, so I had a drink. I had a big drink. I mean, I probably drunk more than I normally ever do. I wanted to go to sleep. I wanted to forget. It worked.

As Professor McConville told the *Sunday Times*:

> We take jurors for granted. There is a lot of talk about public service, but we expose them to extremely distressing events without backup. The trouble is the professionals become case-hardened. They regard jurors as empty shells, as a symbol of the system rather than real human beings.

The victims of crime in the Fuller case included primary victims (the Fullers themselves), secondary victims (the Johnsons and Harry's family) and a range of tertiary victims, potentially including the neighbours and 999 operator who unknowingly heard Nicola being shot, the police who attended at Blackmans Cottage, and the many people, including judges, jurors, lawyers, court staff, experts, journalists and members of the public, who heard the 999 tape at Young's two trials.

But why was the tape played in the courtroom at all? Although it is a rare instance of a live recording of a serious crime in progress, it was far from an ideal window into what happened. The tape did not capture Harry's death or the initial shots fired at Nicola, or anything identifiable about the shooter. It was not directly relevant to the issues in dispute at the trial. However, it was indirectly relevant. It pinpointed the timing of the conclusion of the killings. As well, the early part of the tape laid bare the killer's callousness, which clearly went beyond an initial, possibly reflexive barrage of bullets to a calm, methodical silencing of a terrified and helpless victim some minutes later. It supported the prosecution's theory that Nicola was killed deliberately to ensure that she would not identify her assailant, which in turn suggested that either the killer was known to her or she knew that the killer had an appointment with her husband that morning.

What was more significant was the lengthy portion of the tape after Nicola was shot, where audible sounds of the murders' aftermath were recorded. Often an emergency call tape-recording is a poor way to listen to what is going on in the background. One problem is that the tape captures both ends of the phone call, including both a (typically) panicked caller and a noisy call centre. Indeed (and thankfully), little could be clearly discerned in the first minute of the 999 tape because the sounds were obscured by those of the call centre, picked up via the operator's headset. A second problem is that home phones aren't designed to pick up more distant sounds. The handset Nicola used to place the call could only detect what was happening in or near the couple's bedroom, not elsewhere in the three-storey Blackmans Cottage.

By happenstance, both of these problems were reduced in the last two-thirds of the 999 tape. Just over a minute after the gunshot, the operator muted the call at her end, presumably because no-one was answering her queries and she was attending to other tasks; this meant that the sounds of the centre no longer drowned out the sounds at the caller's end. Just 30 seconds later, there was a further click and breathing could be heard. Apparently, someone had lifted the downstairs handset to see if Nicola had managed to get through to 999. Because the call centre sounds had been muted by then, the killer wrongly thought that the call was never connected. Even more fortuitously, the downstairs handset was left off the hook, perhaps to prevent anyone else calling. The result was that the remainder of the tape contained a reasonable quality audio record of events on both the Cottage's ground and first floors. The tape, and its window into the aftermath of the crime scene, ended three-and-a-half minutes later, when the operator disconnected the call. Noting a 'child on the line', the operator moved on with her day, only to be confronted with the awful truth three weeks later.

The main sounds revealed during those three-and-a-half minutes were of doors and drawers being opened and closed, supporting the prosecution's theory that the motive for the crime was to locate the cash that Harry was said to have hidden in his house. But the handset also caught the sounds of footsteps, which were relevant to another issue in the case: the number of people in the house that morning. On Young's own account, he was in the house at the same time someone else was upstairs, though it is unclear exactly when. As well, the defence drew support for Young's claim of innocence from several witnesses who had reported seeing more than one person acting suspiciously near Blackmans Cottage that morning, contradicting the prosecution's case that the Fullers were the victims of a lone killer.

Again, Young was the beneficiary of the initial police investigation, which began by pursuing 'the theory that there may have been two killers', because of the lack of signs of struggle in the cottage. Early on, Detective Superintendent Graham Hill publicly called for two witnesses to contact the police:

> One was a man who was in Wadhurst just before 7 am on February 10 and the other a woman who twice telephoned in an agitated state on February 17, but never completed her message.

While the woman was merely 'in a distressed state and agitated about whether the killer or killers had been traced', the male witness described 'two men with a cream or yellow Sierra' who walked up the path to Blackmans Cottage, both just over six feet tall and 'smartly dressed'. The *Crimewatch* reconstruction showed a pair of actors entering the cottage, saying 'Hello old son' and Sue Cook, the presenter, added that no-one saw them leave. When announcing a reward for information, Hill suggested that the man may have phoned anonymously because he was in Wadhurst having an affair; he assured the caller that 'any embarrassment would be dealt with sensitively'.

In his letter to Wadhurst residents, he said:

> I am still anxious however to speak to anyone who has not yet been seen by the police, and who was in the vicinity of Blackmans Cottage in the High Street or used the car park to the rear, between 6 am and 10 am on the day of the murders.

To that end, Detective Chief Inspector Alan Snelling spoke to pupils in the assembly hall at Uplands Community College asking them to cast their minds back to the morning of the murder and whether they remembered seeing anything or anyone suspicious—on their way to school—and to see him afterwards. Several did and arrangements were made for detectives to interview them.

At Young's trials, attention focused on two school students who spoke to the police during the investigation's first week. Samantha Coller and Eve Dilworth had left the school that morning to buy some lunch on Wadhurst's high street. Two days after the murders, Coller told police about an event she thought happened just after 9 am. As they walked past Blackmans Cottage, she heard a door slam and then someone bumped into her and she saw someone else standing at the cottage door. Dilworth gave a similar but vaguer statement; she agreed about the slamming door and the person bumping into Coller, but didn't think that the two events happened on the same day.

This evidence put a premium on the footsteps captured on the 999 tape, specifically the number of distinct footsteps, which could cast light on how many people were in Blackmans Cottage immediately after Nicola died. To this end, the prosecution called an expert witness, Christopher Mills, once head of the London police's Audio Laboratory and, in 1994, a consultant on audio forensics. In later years, Mills would advise on such varied cases as the investigation into the disastrous raid on the Branch Davidian compound in Waco, Texas, the judicial inquiry into the Bloody Sunday killings in Northern Ireland and the use of coughs to cheat on the game show *Who Wants to Be a Millionaire?* At Young's trials, Mills testified that, having listened to the tape with special equipment, he could not detect any moment when more than one pair of footsteps could be heard. He conceded, though, that this did not rule out the possibility of two people in the house, albeit one must have been standing still while the other walked.

The defence, unsurprisingly, urged the jury to listen to the tape themselves and see whether or not they agreed with Mills. That meant that the jury in each of Young's trials had to listen to the 999 tape repeatedly.

Channelling the victim

> Had the evening meal. That was fine, bit quiet, and then the pianist come in which was rather nice and he played some jazz and actually it was very good and we had a few drinks and it was funny, 11 o'clock everybody disappeared. Went to their room. It was as if we knew we had to go to bed because we had to get up in the morning and do this thing.

Just under nine months after the Ouija board jurors stayed at *The Old Ship Hotel*, David's jury spent the night of Thursday 15th December 1994 at a London hotel. Young's second jury was amongst the last in England to be put up in overnight accommodation. The prohibition on separating deliberating jurors was lifted in March the following year. According to the media, Blofeld gave special directions about the jurors' hotel stay in Young's retrial:

> Strict controls were placed on the Old Bailey jurors who tried Young for the second time after the Court of Appeal ordered a retrial. They were not allowed any alcohol when they stayed overnight at a hotel on Thursday...

David described the hotel stay three years later:

> We were taken off in a coach right to a hotel and this hotel was actually shut to everybody else. It was just us 12 jurors. We went in the front door and the girl at the desk sort of just smiled as we walked by. Nobody booked in or gave names. We went straight in the lift. Straight upstairs into our rooms. We were given a room and a key each and we were told that dinner would be at 8 and this was sort of quarter past 6, so have a shower and watch a bit of telly in the room. Actually we didn't know but we weren't actually allowed to watch telly. The television we were watching was pre-recorded programmes, not news or something that was actually live. They must have set this up with the hotel.

Despite media claims, David said that alcohol was available to his jury, together with jazz. But there was clearly no holiday camp atmosphere this time. On David's description, the mood was funereal.

Consistently with the Contempt of Court Act, David said nothing on *Modern Times* about how he or other jurors contemplated Young's guilt or innocence. All we know is that, as in Young's first trial, the formal deliberations lasted less than 24 hours and ended with a guilty verdict. But, given David's account, and Blofeld's comment that 'the precise circumstances of Nicola Fuller's death will remain in everybody's mind for years to come', there is something to be gained by speculating about what effect the 999 call would have had on the jurors. While both juries were expected to consider the killer's state of mind as Nicola was killed, and to count footsteps thereafter, it is surely likely that some of them would have spent part of the trial thinking about Nicola herself, specifically her last moments and thoughts. That contemplation would yield a vivid series of images, each more shocking than the last: Nicola hearing the shot that killed her husband; Nicola being shot three times, including through her cheek; Nicola crawling in agony from the hallway to the bedroom to phone for help; Nicola realising that the operator's error meant that help would never come; Nicola's terror as her husband's killer covered her face with a duvet.

The United States legal system, which has many more jury trials than the rest of the world combined, provides an insight into how such emotive thoughts can affect jurors. In 2008, a jury in Montana, hearing a civil action against a doctor for failing to diagnose a man's fatal heart condition, experienced the following closing argument from the plaintiff's lawyer:

> About midnight, 1 o'clock, my heart starts quivering. I don't know what's going on. Then, oh, my God. I'm dying, I think I'm dying. And I just—and that's it. I'm dead. I'm dead. I died. My heart gave out. My little kid came by, kissed me on the cheek. I was dead. Amy came down about an hour later, called my name. I'm dead. I can't get up. She screams. This is horrible. She drags me down onto the floor. She is screaming my name, she is saying,

'Wake up, wake up.' And I'm not — I can't wake up. I'm dead. Amy, I'm dead. She calls 9-1-1.

The lawyer's invented first-person account didn't stop there, instead detailing resuscitation attempts in the ambulance and, eventually, the deceased's autopsy:

> Gosh, he is poking, he is prodding, he is cutting me open, and he's looking at various things. And I hear him say, 'You know, this guy' — he's dictating away 'essentially dies of a — his leaky valve.' And I go, 'A leaky valve? They were supposed to tell me. They were supposed to tell me when I was going to have this replaced. Why didn't they tell me? If I had my valve replaced, I would have been able to see my kids grow up. I would have been able to go to cheerleading with Kaitlin. I would have been able to go to watch these little girls grow up, and I would have been able to walk them down the aisle. And most important, I would have been able to —

JUROR PERRIGO: I'm not okay.

Debbie Perrigo had the good fortune of fainting in the presence, not only of three nurses (who comprised a quarter of her jury) and a former doctor (co-counsel for the plaintiff), but also a currently practising internal medical physician (the defendant in the malpractice suit).

All five leapt to Perrigo's assistance, quickly lowering her head, taking her pulse and history, and calling 911 so that she could be taken to hospital to monitor her heart palpitations. The defendant later advised the judge:

> I think she is he going to be fine. I think she just had a vasovagal attack, a near syncopal attack. I think she was emotional, a little bit distraught. I think Mr. Hammond gave a very powerful closing statement. I think she really put herself in the position of Mr. Heidt, and I think she just — she's a very empathetic lady.

After Perrigo was replaced by an alternate and the attorney notified his insurer, the trial continued and the jury dismissed the plaintiff's claim.

However, the Montana Supreme Court held that the doctor's commendable actions in assisting an ill juror prejudiced the jury in her own favour and ordered a retrial. The new jury awarded Amy Heidt $1.7 million.

It turns out that this sort of jury address is fairly common in American malpractice suits. Former Vice Presidential nominee (and later disgraced Presidential candidate) John Edwards used a similar technique in his days as a trial lawyer, on one occasion narrating the experiences of an unborn baby in a case where a doctor was accused of waiting too long to conduct a caesarean. The brain-damaged toddler, he told the jury 'is inside me, and she's talking to you'. While the Montana Supreme Court didn't comment on this advocacy technique in Heidt's appeal, the same court later dealt with its use in a criminal trial, where a teenage babysitter was accused of shaking her charge. The prosecutor opened her argument as follows:

> What a difference a day makes. Before June 11th of 2008, I was a normal, healthy, happy kid. My parents and I had hopes and dreams for me. This is me on June 1st of 2008 at my sister Anastasia's birthday party. After June 11th of 2008, I would never ever, ever be the same again. My life and the lives of my family would be drastically changed forever because of what my baby-sitter, the Defendant, did to me.

She went on to describe, in the first person and interspersed with photos, the babysitter's alleged assault and the infant's struggles to walk and talk in later years, concluding when the boy himself was wheeled into the courtroom. After the babysitter was convicted and sentenced to 15 years in prison, a majority of the appeal court upheld her conviction because her counsel did not object to the prosecutor's speech at the trial.

However, in a lengthy dissent, Justice Laurie McKinnon, known for her work with disabled and abused children, condemned the prosecutor's advocacy:

> 'Channelling the victim' is a technique by which a lawyer speaks to the jury in the first person as though she is the injured or deceased person. It is calculated to produce a dramatic and emotional impact on the jury by bringing

to life in the courtroom a dead victim or a victim who — as here — cannot testify. In my view, a prosecutor who channels an eight-month-old infant, states that 'I can't tell my mom I love her,' and asks the jury to 'tell [the infant] that you heard him' has engaged in misconduct calling into doubt the fundamental fairness of the trial itself.

She described the approach as 'a form of unsworn, unchecked testimony'.

The playing of the 999 tape in Stephen Young's trial was not unsworn testimony, because Nicola said nothing in support of either side's case. Nor was it unchecked; the tape was no fiction and both sides made legitimate use of its contents. But, as the distressed juror in Young's first trial and David's account from the second trial clearly show, the tape was likely to 'produce a dramatic and emotional impact on the jury by bringing to life in the courtroom a dead victim who cannot testify'. Empathetic listeners would experience Nicola's hopelessness and terror in the last moments of her life, potentially over and over. And they would surely 'channel' some of her last thoughts. As her father later said: 'It is horrific to think that in her time of need it was obvious nobody was coming'. Indeed, part of the tragedy is that it was probably Nicola's bravery and perseverance that alerted the killer that she was still alive. As Michael Lawson pointed out to David's jury: 'The killer may have been forgiven for thinking that having shot her three times, she was dead'. Had Nicola lain still until the killer or killers left, she may have been able to communicate successfully with the operator, allowing her both to survive and identify her husband's assailant.

Because the 12 jurors' affidavits remain largely unpublished (and probably didn't touch on the jurors' emotional reactions to the evidence), we know nothing of the impact of the 999 tape on Adrian's jury, the first to convict Young. But it is possible that the actions of the four jurors at *The Old Ship* were in part due to their thinking about Nicola's dying moments. Those moments and, especially, her failed attempts to speak as she died, provide a ready explanation for why the topic of speaking with the dead came up at the hotel dinner there. More speculatively, the contents of the 999 tape may explain why the four jurors chose (if that is what they did) to speak, not with Nicola (who saw her killer's face) but Harry (who was shot from behind). The very thought of listening to Nicola's words from beyond the grave would surely have been too awful to contemplate.

Each one alone

> And at that point every juror was crying. Every juror, there's tears coming out of their face. They just … this was it. This was the bit they didn't want to do. This was the bit they couldn't cope with and they knew you can't change your mind.

The first half of the 1990s marked a new awareness of the stress some jurors experience. In the USA, this recognition arose in 1992 after the trial of serial killer Jeffrey Dahmer, where the evidence was so graphic that the judge arranged for mental health professionals to offer a post-verdict debriefing to the jurors; all 14 accepted. Two years later (the week before the Ouija board story broke), the USA Centre for Jury Studies drew on subsequent debriefing experiences to suggest that modern technology was adding to juror stress:

> Rather than having the chalkmarks on the pavement as to where the body was, you've now got a videotape — a color videotape.

Indeed, as has long been the norm, both of Young's juries were shown 'a grisly video of the crime scene which showed the victim's bodies as they were discovered by the police'.

The following year, 1995, proved to be a bellwether one for the nascent field of juror stress, with the trials of O J Simpson in Los Angeles, serial killer and rapist Paul Bernardo in Toronto and serial killer Rosemary West in Winchester, the first in England where jurors were offered counselling. The West case came too late for Stephen Young's jurors — the first of the bodies in West's 'House of Horrors' was found two days after Adrian's jury was empanelled. And, in any case, the recognition that juror stress is not limited to the most horrific crimes or high-profile trials was still years away.

Instead, trial judges micro-managed the emotional consequences of trials ad hoc. For example, in the trial of Paul Esslemont for the strangling and beating of a three-year-old, the trial judge modified the evidence before the court to protect the jurors:

> Those photographs had been considered by those who prepared the documents to be of a horrific nature. Accordingly, the photograph which was shown to the jury of the little boy's body in position in the foliage had had a small piece of yellow paper approximately one inch or three-quarters of an inch square, put over the face. It left the photograph sufficiently clear for the jury to be able to see the position in which the body lay and what were its surroundings.

However, the trial judge, recognising that the wounds on the toddler's face may be relevant to disputes in the case about the blood on Esslemont's golf club and shoes, told the jury:

> When you retire a copy of the photographs in their full form will go with you. You do not have to look at them if you do not require to do so, but it may be that some of you will want to, particularly when you come to consider the vitally important matter about where blood might fly and so on. It might be said in not seeing that you were handicapped in it and if at least some of you, those of you who feel able to do so, can look at it and be sure that they know about it, so much the better, but no-one is insisting if you find it too impossible that you have to do so, as long as you listen to those amongst your number who do.

After he was convicted, Esslemont argued that the trial judge had struck the wrong balance between the jurors' fact-finding role and the emotional consequences of that role, because the jury would be divided between those who lifted the little yellow square and those who didn't. Lord Chief Justice Peter Taylor rejected the argument:

We do not consider that the criminal justice process requires that kind of absolutism. We consider that the approach that the learned judge adopted here was a reasonable approach, and we do not think that there was an irregularity.

Taylor added, having looked at the photo himself, that the hidden portion 'cannot have made any difference to their deliberations'.

After the O J Simpson verdict, *The Mirror* noted the onerous conditions imposed on the jury during that trial:

And the O J Twelve lived under unusually strict rules—NO locked doors to their rooms, NO booze and NO small gatherings. They were either all together or each one alone.

Mr Justice Blofeld reportedly imposed much the same conditions on the jury at Young's retrial. David described how the jury coped after delivering their verdict:

We went into the jurors' room again and everyone's sitting there sobbing. It was…for five weeks nobody had had any physical contact but there was people cuddling, there was holding hands, there was people saying goodbye and we were actually in that room for an hour before we could compose ourselves enough to actually leave the court.

The end of hotel stays a few months later would allow jurors to seek the solace of their families and friends while they deliberated. However, section 8 of the Contempt of Court Act meant—and still means—that English jurors cannot lawfully talk about their actual deliberations to anyone, including family and psychologists.

We are left to speculate about Adrian's jury, the first to convict Young. It is at least possible that events at *The Old Ship*—from the drinking to the jokes to the dinner talk of séances to the clandestine gathering to, even, the makeshift Ouija board—were methods the jurors used to cope with the stresses of the trial and the horrific evidence. Perhaps the 'holiday camp atmosphere' described by Adrian (who said he felt isolated from the group because of his youth) was a cover for deeper emotional difficulties some of the other (maybe more empathetic) jurors were experiencing. And, perhaps, going through the motions — physical and mental — of the séance with one of the murder victims was yet another method of processing their emotional turmoil. The same may be true of their decision to plan a reunion a year later.

Less speculatively, David's account casts new light on a piece of evidence about the Ouija board jurors that the Court of Appeal thought was highly significant to its decision to order a retrial:

> The three women jurors were upset about what emerged. One was crying and took the view that it had gone too far. Why, if it was just a game?

Adrian himself told the *News of the World* that, when the verdict was delivered:

> I felt really guilty. The women on the jury started crying. I think they realised how serious it was. I felt distressed putting someone away for life

And all of David's jury sobbed for an hour after they delivered their verdict. Clearly, none of these events was a game. But nor were the jurors' tears in *The Old Ship* a reliable guide to whether they were experiencing a spiritual epiphany or simply deep distress.

The choice

> The first week I felt good. I felt I've got over this and then I kept having nightmares about it and I said to my wife that I had a nightmare. She said 'Oh, you've had a nightmare', she says, 'We've had a nightmare living with you.'

A few months after the *Modern Times* documentary, the juror who sat on the trial of Paul Esslemont identified herself as Ann Routley. She revealed that, after she visited the playground where the toddler died, she spoke to locals who told her that they didn't believe that Esslemont was the killer. Eventually, she contacted the defendant's lawyer and his family, even visiting Esslemont in prison, and began to campaign for his exoneration.

On the eve of the Court of Appeal's reconsideration of its earlier ruling upholding the teenager's conviction, she told the *Evening Standard*:

> In the jury room we had the choice to see pictures without the masking tape. I decided to look at these. There was a sense that all this had happened and it had to be faced. You can't hide it and you can't try to protect yourself from the fact that people do these things, and these pictures show the consequences. You have the intelligence to be detached, but there is this sense of being trapped on the jury and that you have to make a decision. The judge put a heavy burden on us by saying, in effect: 'If you say he is guilty when he is innocent there's a killer on the loose—and if you say he is innocent when he is guilty there's a killer on the loose'.

This time, the Court of Appeal allowed the appeal, relying on evidence that Esslemont had his golf club with him when he guided a police officer through grass where the child's body was later found, as well a fresh expert analysis of the photo of the toddler's face, which showed parallel marks on the boy's face that could not have been caused by a golf club. Consistent with the Contempt of Court Act, Routley never revealed whether she was one of the ten jurors who had convicted the teen or one of the pair who would have acquitted him.

David, at least, has not suffered the burden of having been found to have imposed a miscarriage of justice on Stephen Young. But the same isn't true for the four hotel room jurors. As Michael Johnson told the media on the day the Court of Appeal ordered a retrial:

> The jurors have made a complete joke of our daughter's death. Anyone who sits on a jury and can lark around like this must be absolutely sick. After listening to all the evidence, I hope it haunts them.

Nicola's grieving parents will narrate the aftermath of the Ouija board case.

The Ouija Board Jurors

CHAPTER 7

Such a Fearful Spectre

> First blush — Various newspaper headlines — Strange circumstances — A lighter tale — Such a stupid thing — Jekyll and Hyde — The pain is still here.

On the Sunday before the second anniversary of Harry and Nicola Fuller's deaths, Nicola's parents sat down to watch the BBC's long-running religious programme, *Songs of Praise*. Hosted that evening by comedian Sir Harry Secombe, it was a special broadcast from Wormwood Scrubs, a Category B prison in west-London for adult men classified as non-dangerous but a potential escape risk. Barbara Johnson told the media:

> We were so shocked to see Stephen Young on the programme. We always find Songs of Praise quite uplifting, then I looked up and saw him for the first time in some months — we were too shocked to turn it off.

The former Pembury Player was once again singing before an audience, probably for the first time since his turn as Ali Baba. It was not the last time his image would haunt Nicola's parents.

A BBC spokesman later said that he was sorry to hear of the Johnsons' distress, but pointed out that 'the prisoner concerned was not interviewed in the programme — he appeared in general shots as one of around 40 prisoners'. Barbara Johnson responded that *Songs of Praise* had 'brought the sadness back for the family':

The Home Secretary is supposed to be cutting down on crime and helping victims more, but this isn't helping victims by showing what they do in prison — they have too much of a good time there. Harry Secombe said he could walk away from the gates of the prison, but we can never walk away and we will live a life sentence.

The details of the Johnsons' life sentence by then included more than just the facts of Nicola's death. A year earlier, at the end of Young's first trial, Michael Johnson had declared: 'It is the end of the chapter, but not the end of the book. We have good days and bad days'. His metaphor was all too accurate. Several weeks later, news broke of the jurors' makeshift Ouija board.

This final chapter tracks the public impact of the Ouija board case, from its first revelation in an English tabloid, through the media's scrutiny of Young's appeal and re-trial, and in its lengthy aftermath as a recurring footnote in discussions of the jury system. In this chapter, I also set out my own views on what I think happened at both Blackmans Cottage and *The Old Ship*.

First blush

> We had started to rebuild our lives, but I don't know if I can go through it all again. I am still in a state of shock — it is unbelievable.

The Johnsons most likely learned what four jurors did at the trial of the alleged killer of their daughter the same way almost everyone else did: by reading the now defunct English tabloid, the *News of the World*.

The top half of the Sunday tabloid's front page on 17th April 1994 featured a photo of a crouching, skimpily clothed woman and the teaser: 'World Exclusive: Sly's Cheating on Fiancée with Me!' Below the fold was a smaller teaser for a 'Royal Exclusive: Margaret's secret affair with film star'. The rest of the lower half of the page was dominated by a massive three-line headline: 'MURDER JURY'S OUIJA BOARD

VERDICT'. The Johnsons would have seen Young's 'smile of a killer', alongside unsmiling pictures of the alleged adulterers Sylvester Stallone and the Countess of Snowdon. A cryptic banner at the bottom of the page promised 'Free Seeds for Every Reader'.

The first published account of the story of the Ouija board jurors commenced:

> A killer may be freed after sensational claims that jurors used a ouija board hours before finding him guilty of a double murder. One worried juror has sworn a statement that three of his colleagues held a secret late-night séance to contact Stephen Young's victims.

This paragraph had multiple inaccuracies—the word 'hours' (there were at least 12), 'sworn' (Adrian's letter wasn't even signed), 'three' (there were four), 'secret' (not for long) and 'victims' (the Ouija board only purported to contact Harry)—in part reflecting Adrian's own misunderstandings. As well, the headline's reference to a 'jury', and the implications that there was an actual 'board' and that it determined the 'verdict' initiated a pattern of standard misconceptions about the case that persists decades later.

But the article was entirely accurate to claim that it was an 'EXCLUSIVE by Gary Jones, Crime Reporter'. Unlike the Stallone affair (a story that broke a month earlier) and Princess Margaret's (the subject of years of open speculation by then), the *News of the World*'s Ouija board story was a genuine exclusive, revealing the events in *The Old Ship* beyond the jurors' and Young's circles for the first and (until the court hearings) only time. Notably (and exceptionally for accounts of alleged juror misbehaviour), the exclusivity extended to the nation's courts. Young's lawyers didn't send Adrian's claims to Lewes Crown Court until several days later. It is likely that England's judges, including the Lord Chief Justice, first heard about Adrian's account by reading (or being told about) Jones' article in the *News of the World*.

Such exclusive revelations about jurors have been legally dangerous in England since 1981, when the Contempt of Court Act was enacted. Official confirmation of that danger for newspapers came just three weeks before Young's first trial. Two years earlier, the *Mail on Sunday* had published statements from three jurors who sat in the Blue Arrow trial, a notorious and largely failed fraud prosecution of merchant bankers who allegedly bought shares in one of their own clients while they readied it for a takeover. The paper's account included a lengthy justification for the decision to publish the jurors' words, which concluded:

> At a time when the role of juries is being investigated by the Royal Commission on Criminal Justice, our transcripts show an intelligence and application that will surprise the jurors' critics. Far from diminishing respect for our criminal justice system, which the Contempt Act seeks to uphold, they enhance it. This report is the first real look at how juries do their work in this country. We publish it because it shows that justice is available through the jury system in our courts—something which in recent months has been in dispute. That is the public interest argument for publication.

When it was prosecuted for contempt, the *Mail* offered a different, technical argument: that the newspaper didn't 'disclose' the jurors' deliberations; rather, it was the jurors themselves who did the disclosing, by speaking to (unidentified) American researchers, who in turn handed the interview transcripts to the tabloid. Early in February 1994, the House of Lords rejected that argument, ruling that the statute's ban on disclosure applied no matter how many hands the information passed through first, unless the information was already public knowledge. After focussing on a handful of negative remarks about some jurors (such as the claim that one fell asleep during the trial), the Lords upheld £60,000 in fines for the contempt.

The *News of the World's* Ouija board exclusive, published ten weeks after the House of Lords ruling, offered no justifications, legal or otherwise. The article's public interest was the exact opposite of the *Mail's*: a sharp critique of the jury system. As for its legality, that was only settled two months later when the Court of Appeals ruled that hotel room events aren't covered at all by the Contempt of Court Act, whether they are disclosed to courts or newspaper readers. The British Press Awards named Jones its 'Reporter of the Year' in early 1995, although that is most likely due to his exposé of Princess Diana's phone harassment of a married art dealer later in 1994. Five years later, he was the subject of a landmark ruling in the House of Lords requiring him to identify who had given him the confidential hospital records of Moors murderer Ian Brady. A decade after, he was the editor of the *Sunday Mirror* and *People*.

How did Jones scoop England's courts on the Ouija board jurors? The only published account of how Adrian's tale became public is set out in the Court of Appeal's judgement:

> What had occurred in the hotel had caused one juror such concern that he consulted a solicitor to whom he gave a handwritten statement in early April 1994. The solicitor consulted counsel who spoke to leading counsel for the appellant. The application before this court on 13 June 1994 for leave to appeal was based upon the juror's written statement.

This does not reveal how (or even the fact that) the information reached the *News of the World* first. It is obvious that either Adrian (or his family) or Young (or his lawyers) spoke with Jones sometime in mid-April. Given that both Young's solicitor and Adrian ultimately went on the record with the tabloid, the most likely scenario is that both agreed in some way to Jones' scoop.

In Adrian's case, he may have wanted his story to be publicly disclosed as soon as possible to ease his troubled conscience. But other things may also motivate an unemployed 22-year-old to speak to the media, especially a tabloid. Piers Morgan was the editor of *News of the World* at the time, but his successor Phil Hall recently claimed credit for Jones' scoop. An article in 2015 about his later career as a public relations consultant canvassed his views on the controversies that had recently enveloped the newspaper industry:

> In recent years 34 journalists have been arrested and/or charged on suspicion of paying public officials for [a] story. Two convictions currently stand. Hall freely admits that he signed off such payments in his time as an editor. 'Journalists must be allowed to pay sources otherwise you won't get the story. We had a prison officer came to us and said we could buy the key to

the prison. He's a public official. He said people were being allowed into the prison, bringing in stuff—drugs and alcohol—and they had sold the key to some of these criminal associates. We paid him £500, tested the key and walked in and ran it as a front page splash in the News of the World.' Another such story involved paying a juror who revealed that a jury reached their verdict by using a ouija board.

While this seems to be the only public suggestion that Adrian was paid for speaking to the tabloid, supporting clues appear in the original articles. Jones' interview with the juror repeatedly mentions that Adrian was unemployed and quotes him as saying:

> It's not that I wanted to snitch on other jury members, who were nice people, but in the interests of justice all this had to come out. I hope I don't have to go through anything like this again. I haven't been able to concentrate on looking for a job.

This circumstance may provide a justification of sorts (if one was needed) if money did change hands. Despite the widespread interest in the story, Adrian has seemingly never spoken to any other outlet.

In the case of Young and his lawyers, there is only a very indirect hint of their possible motivations. While Young's appeal was being heard, the regular column 'The Sharp End' in the June 1994 edition of legal practitioners' journal *The Lawyer*, commenced:

> Because of section 8 of the Contempt of Court Act 1981 I am forbidden from telling you the circumstances that led up to a jury finding my client, Stephen Young, with the aid of a Ouija board, guilty of a double murder. This device was apparently used to make contact with one of the deceased victims...

Consistently with the pattern of misdescription initiated in the *News of the World*, Young's solicitor Stephen Gilchrist describes the jurors' glass and paper as a 'device' used to 'aid' the 'jury'. He goes on to add:

Unsurprisingly, when this information leaked out, the first port of call was the Court of Appeal, which initially had to decide whether it was itself constrained by the legislation from investigating the evidence of what, at first blush, suggests the possibility of a monstrous miscarriage of justice. This evidence emanated from within and without the jury room.

Young's lawyers would have been well aware that the Court of Appeal could simply refuse to hear or investigate Adrian's account because of Mansfield's rule, the Contempt of Court Act or appeal judges' scepticism about jurors' post-verdict allegations. Surely it would have crossed the lawyers' minds that, if 'this information leaked out' to the public ahead of the appeal, then Young's chances of overturning his convictions could increase. Indeed, applying the House of Lords reasoning in the Blue Arrow case, the prior publication meant that the contempt statute no longer barred the court from being informed of Adrian's claims.

Various newspaper headlines

> People have sometimes got away with things because someone has screwed up on a jury.

We can only speculate on Stephen Young's initial response to Adrian's claims, whether he heard of them via *News of the World* or, more likely, from his lawyers at Wormwood Scrubs. What is clear is that he eventually came to see the claims as an opportunity to escape, not just his existing murder convictions, but any future prosecution for the Fullers' deaths.

His lawyers pursued that goal the moment the Court of Appeal allowed the broker's appeal:

THE LORD CHIEF JUSTICE: Mr Penry-Davey, we have decided that the appeal must be allowed in this case. I assume, Mr Lawson, you wish the case to be re-tried?

MR LAWSON: Yes.

THE LORD CHIEF JUSTICE: Can you argue against that?

MR PENRY-DAVEY: My Lord, I do seek to address you.

THE LORD CHIEF JUSTICE: Very well.

MR PENRY-DAVEY: My Lord there are files available for the court.

The transcript states that the barrister then read out 'various newspapers headlines' to the Court of Appeal and summarises David Penry-Davey's argument: 'that because of both national and international publicity which had followed the original hearing it was impossible for the appellant to receive a fair trial if a re-trial were to be ordered'.

Young's original trial received understandable local publicity, including, after his late-March 1994 conviction, harsh takes such as the 'smile of a killer' headline, speculation about his psychopathy and the harrowing evidence about Nicola's 999 call. But Penry-Davey's reference to 'international publicity' implies that his concerns also extended to media coverage of the Ouija board incident, which was picked up by all national papers and several international news agencies. Penry-Davey's argument did not need to rest on the Jones *News of the World* pieces. The appeal hearings themselves were comprehensively covered by the media in mid-1994.

The issue of reporting Adrian's claims was first raised with the court at the end of the initial appeal hearing:

MR PENRY-DAVEY: My Lord, I am not instructed on behalf of the media, but I am asked to enquire whether it would be proper for the newspapers to report allegations that have already been made in the press?

THE LORD CHIEF JUSTICE: I think all one can say is that what took place this morning was in open court. I think anything that has been said in court today can be reported, but so far as anything else is concerned, the press must consider their position.

MR PENRY-DAVEY: My Lord, I am happy in the knowledge that in so far as anything was said, it was said by your Lordship and not by me!

Penry-Davey's stance deftly shifted responsibility for any publicity about the appeal to the court itself. The Court of Appeal's response seemingly relied on the effect of the Contempt of Court Act as so recently outlined by the House of Lords, including the permission to publish courtroom disclosures.

The court could have imposed its own ban on publicity of the Ouija board allegations, but didn't. This may be because neither party asked, the *News of the World* had already published Adrian's account, or the Court of Appeal wanted to ensure that the public learnt about how the justice system was responding to the incident. The only public commentary the judges did criticise was the missive by Young's solicitor calling for reform to the Contempt of Court Act:

THE LORD CHIEF JUSTICE: The one matter, Mr Penry-Davey, that I must draw to your attention is an article which appears in The Lawyer for 19 July. Have you seen it?

MR PENRY-DAVEY: I have, my Lord, yes.

THE LORD CHIEF JUSTICE: Each member of this court is disturbed by that article. It was written by a solicitor who, I think, is instructing you, is that right?

MR PENRY-DAVEY: Yes, my Lord.

THE LORD CHIEF JUSTICE: Certainly it is open to the construction that it deals with matters which could prejudice the administration of justice because after all, if this case did proceed any further it may not—it may not—only be the Court of Appeal that would be looking at it, it might be another jury. Looking at that first paragraph, for example—not to mention any other paragraphs in it—we think there are matters there which ought to be looked at by the Attorney General.

There is no record of official proceedings, charges or punishments arising from Taylor's reference of Stephen Gilchrist to the Attorney-General.

As for Penry-Davey's later argument against Young facing a re-trial, the Lord Chief Justice dismissed it out of hand:

No, Mr Penry-Davey, we are all three agreed that there should be a re-trial here. That being so, the order of the court is that the appeal will be allowed and the conviction quashed. There will be a re-trial on a fresh indictment which will be preferred by the direction of this court. It will be tried at the Central Criminal Court [i.e. the Old Bailey].

The order to switch from Hove Crown Court to London's Old Bailey for the re-trial is not explained, but was presumably designed to minimise the impact of local publicity in Sussex (and, perhaps, the embarrassing possibility that Young's new jury would be put up in *The Old Ship*). Penry-Davey immediately told the Court of Appeal that 'it would be unfortunate if there were reporting of extensive detail following this hearing', because the Ouija board purported to reveal the 'identity of the murderer'. Taylor's response was to order the 'postponement' of any publication of the contents of the jurors' affidavits, including anything revealed in the Court of Appeal's own judgement, to avoid 'a substantial risk of prejudice' to Young. His order was expressed to extend to 'until after the re-trial *or any appeal there may be following that*' (emphasis added), inadvertently adding a decade to its effect.

Taylor's order could not have guaranteed the fairness of Young's re-trial, for four reasons. First, the order did not prevent publication of what was already said in the earlier hearings. Second, the new trial in the Old Bailey was scheduled almost immediately, less than a month after his appeal was allowed and far too soon for memories of the earlier publicity about the Ouija board jurors to fade. And, third, 'the identity of the murderer' purportedly revealed by the séance was obvious to everyone.

Indeed, *The Times* felt free to report on the makeshift Ouija board's claim the day after the Court of Appeal imposed its ban:

> While the jury was staying overnight at a hotel, they had tried to consult the victim during a 'drunken experiment'. They asked, 'Who did it?', and were allegedly told that the defendant, Stephen Young, was responsible.

As well, Taylor himself made it clear that the basic facts of the Ouija board case could always be published:

> THE LORD CHIEF JUSTICE: It cannot prejudice you, can it, if it is the mere fact that this court has allowed the appeal on the basis of what happened with the jury at the hotel?
>
> MR PENRY-DAVEY: No.

Penry-Davey was, perhaps, simply acknowledging the impossibility of putting that particular cat back in the bag, in light of the *News of the World* article and subsequent reporting of the hearing.

There is no doubt that Young's new jury was well aware of the 'basic facts' described by Taylor. Mr Justice Blofeld expressly told them:

> The original trial of Stephen Young for these murders took place in March, 1994, at Hove Crown Court. The defendant was convicted. It emerged subsequently that irregularities concerning the use of a ouija board by the jury had occurred. The Court of Appeal quashed the convictions and ordered a retrial.

As usual, this account referred to a 'jury', rather than jurors, and potentially left unclear that the incident occurred at a hotel, rather than in a jury room, and involved only a glass and paper. Regardless, the fact that the broker had not only been convicted by his earlier jury, but had his conviction quashed because of the behaviour of those same jurors (rather than an error by one of the court officers or a flaw in the evidence) was expressly brought to his new jury's attention. Some of David's jury may well have recognised that their verdict could be seen as determining, not only Young's guilt or innocence, but also (if they acquitted Young) that he might have owed his earlier conviction to a séance.

Strange circumstances

> It was hard enough to go through the trial last time, but this time it will be unbearable.

Years later, the Johnsons disclosed that their 'biggest fear at the re-trial was he was going to walk out. It still feels as if we're being stalked by him from prison'.

Stephen Young's re-trial could never be a mere replay of his first trial. A different trial judge potentially meant different rulings about the evidence. For example, one issue in both trials was a notice of alibi lodged by Young's solicitor in August 1993 in the following terms:

> Mr Young's contention will be that he was not at the house at Blackmans Cottage at the time that the murders were committed although at the moment it is not possible to be specific as to his exact whereabouts.

This notice sits poorly with Young's testimony in both trials that he was in Wadhurst when the Fullers were killed and was inside the house very shortly after. But Young insisted that he never authorised the lodging of the alibi. In his first trial, Mr Justice French ruled that this meant that the jury could not see the notice. But Mr Justice Blofeld, at Young's second trial, let the jury see it, albeit warning them to disregard it unless they were sure that Young authorised it.

Both sides' lawyers were also free to act differently at the re-trial, and would inevitably learn from the earlier proceeding. Young's prosecutors would, presumably, want to repeat the arguments that (seemingly) succeeded at the first trial, but could also shift to accommodate Young's defence, including his new account of the events of 10th February 1993 and the threats he later received. Young's lawyers, by contrast, had reason to alter their earlier (seemingly) unsuccessful strategy. For example, Penry-Davey opted not to call Young's character witnesses the second time round. So much, so typical of re-trials. What was less typical in the Ouija board case was that, despite the very short time between Young's first and second trials (nine months) and the renewal of legal aid (ordered by the Court of Appeal), his defence team at his second trial was missing a key member.

As with Sir Christopher French and Lord Chief Justice Peter Taylor, Young's first trial and appeal preceded a sharp reversal in the fortunes of Young's solicitor. Stephen Gilchrist first met Young in May 1993, shortly after the broker's arrest. Although Young already had a legal aid lawyer by then, he agreed to have his file and legal aid certificate transferred to Gilchrist Solicitors. Aged 44 at the time, Gilchrist had practised as a criminal lawyer for nearly 20 years. While he spent most of that time employed by a criminal law firm, Hart Fortgang, eventually as one of three equity partners, he had recently started his own practice with his cousin, a commercial lawyer. At the same time, he became president of England's Legal Aid Practitioners Group, greatly lifting his media profile. As well, he was the moving spirit of a novel scheme allowing private criminal lawyers to arrange for after-hours calls from police stations to be diverted to solicitors willing to work at night, who would provide on-the-spot advice and a referral to the daytime lawyer. Gilchrist led a court challenge to the refusal of the Legal Aid Board (which ran a competing duty solicitor scheme of its own) to fund the night-time lawyers. His challenge succeeded in the same week Young was arrested and, in a major victory, the Board's own appeal was dismissed one week before Young's first trial.

Alas, 1994 was also the year that Gilchrist's career started to fall apart. The basic problem was that, while Gilchrist was a successful lawyer and his new firm had plenty of paying clients, he was a poor administrator. He failed to manage the billing of his new firm and found himself increasingly short of cash. In the second half of 1994, he was squeezed by both his bankers, who lowered his overdraft, and his former partners, who pursued him over a £160,000 deficit left over from his earlier business. At the same time, his marriage faltered, with he and his wife separating temporarily in January 1995 and again a year later. Unsurprisingly, his health suffered.

In December 1994, as Young was being retried, Gilchrist sought help from his doctor who referred him to the Priory Clinic in London, a hospital for stress and anxiety, where he received psychotherapy and treatment over the next two years. The result was that Gilchrist was not present for any of Young's re-trial in late-1994, replaced instead by his 'outdoor clerk'. Young was still represented by his earlier barrister, David Penry-Davey QC, but the absence of his main instructing solicitor had at least a mildly negative effect on the broker's defence. For example, when an issue arose in the trial about when Young first told his lawyers that he supplied a Walther PPK to Harry, his clerk was unable to find the relevant paperwork and Gilchrist, when phoned, couldn't remember, so Penry-Davey (reluctant to ask Young himself on the stand) opted not to clarify the issue before the jury.

After Young was convicted a second time, his relationship with his solicitor broke down completely. In Wormwood Scrubs, Young met one of Gilchrist's repeat clients, who was likewise convicted of murder in a 1994 trial at Hove Crown Court. Colin Waters had a string of dishonesty offences, but no convictions for violence until his 17-month-old stepson was beaten to death while Waters was staying over. Although Waters blamed the child's mother, he was convicted based on pathology evidence that the child died when he was alone with Waters. After losing his own appeal, he accused Gilchrist of conspiring with the courts against him. In turn, Young soon claimed that Gilchrist handled his own case incompetently by failing to identify evidence, interview witnesses or manage the paperwork. The pair sacked him and then accused their ex-solicitor of illegally retaining some of their case documents.

The perfect storm of these two difficult clients and his personal troubles ultimately derailed Gilchrist's career. Believing that he had transferred all of Young's and Waters' files to them by the end of 1995, Gilchrist ignored repeated requests for the documents from their new lawyer and, eventually, the Solicitors' Complaints Bureau. He later explained that he had assumed that his former clients were simply harassing him and that he had plenty of other problems to deal with. His cousin had left his firm in 1996, leaving behind unfinished cases and unpaid disbursements, just as Gilchrist faced a bankruptcy petition from the English customs service over unpaid taxes. Scrambling to bring his affairs into order, he hired a new employee solicitor (who soon quit) and a practice manager, before going briefly bankrupt in early 1997. Although the bankruptcy was quickly annulled, Gilchrist lost his right to practice alone. In September of that year, he faced a lawsuit from Waters and Young over their missing documents. Representing himself in the Central London County Court, he revealed that he had searched his office and found a box of papers from the Fuller case and undertook to forward all the remaining documents to Young's new solicitor. Alas, his new practice manager failed to send all the documents and Gilchrist was left to personally deliver another box he belatedly found at the end of 1997.

Gilchrist's career reached its nadir five years after the Ouija board case, when the Solicitors Disciplinary Tribunal pursued him over a string of allegations, ranging from breaching his undertaking to the court and failing to deliver Young's and Waters' papers, to being late in paying his cousin's barristers and filing his accountancy reports, thriftily using an out-of-date letterhead that wrongly claimed he was allowed to conduct investments and, repeatedly, ignoring, disobeying and even misleading the Complaints Bureau itself. Gilchrist admitted most of the misconduct, but threw himself at the tribunal's mercy, citing his personal troubles, his subsequent repayment of all of his debts, his new employment at a large firm and his two difficult clients, including how Young's,

> original conviction in the murder trial had been set aside in somewhat strange circumstances. It had been discovered that the Jury had used a 'Oji' board to assist in its deliberations.

(This summary by the tribunal of course contains the usual misstatements of the case's facts).

In late-1998, the tribunal rebuffed Gilchrist's offer to pay a hefty fine and instead suspended him from practice for a year. Worse soon followed. After he unsuccessfully appealed that punishment, the tribunal found him guilty of a much more serious allegation: mixing his clients' money with his firm's. While the tribunal accepted that Gilchrist's mistake was due to poor management, rather than dishonesty, and no clients lost money, it nevertheless suspended his licence for a further four years. A successful appeal in 2001 brought his ordeal to an end in 2002, coincidentally the same year Young's second appeal against his murder convictions was first heard.

Earth-bound evidence

> The whole episode has put us right back where we were a year ago.

True to Lord Taylor's order, the media generally refrained from mentioning the details of the Ouija board incident during Young's four-week re-trial in November and December 1994. However, in late-November, the *Sunday Times* used the hook (inaccurate as to both the process and the substance of Young's appeal) that 'last week, a trial restarted after a jury had been dismissed for using a ouija board' to run a ludicrous feature article.

'Things That Go Bump' described a pseudonymous 14-year-old living in an isolated cottage in the 'Weald of Kent' who used a (real) Ouija board to communicate with her recently dead father. After the board crudely revealed to all that the she had lost her virginity, the household was affected by misbehaving record players and pets, and unexplained bumps and screams, only stopping when a parish priest sprinkled holy water everywhere. The article's supposed author, the teen's mother, concluded:

> I have had many experiences in life, but this was quite the most terrifying of all. My daughter vowed that she would never use a Ouija board again, and hasn't. Or so she says.

If a juror in Young's re-trial took this account seriously, then it would imply that the broker's previous jury had dabbled in powers beyond their control.

Such a Fearful Spectre

When Young was convicted a second time—and probably while David's jury were still sobbing in the jury room—local and overseas newspapers announced the new 'Ouija board verdict'. Reuters reported:

> A murder verdict by a British jury which tried to contact the spirit world was upheld on Friday…The retrial jury found enough earth-bound evidence to convict Young of the killings. An Ouija-board is an oblong piece of wood, inscribed with letters of the alphabet, used in séances. Spirits supposedly control a pointer which spells out the answer to questions asked by participants.

As usual, the media's account wrongly implied that all 12 jurors in the first trial had used a real Ouija board that one of them brought to the deliberations. The media's point in saying that 'earth-bound evidence' had reached the same result as using an 'oblong piece of wood' was that the story of the Ouija board jurors was one of mere juror foolishness, rather than a false verdict. Young, though, maintained his innocence, telling Blofeld: 'I didn't do it, my Lord'. A member of the public retorted: 'You did it all right, you bugger—rot'. Young would not have a chance to contest that retort for a decade.

While Young's first appeal was brought before the Court of Appeal extremely quickly, his second was extremely slow, probably in part because of his troubles with Stephen Gilchrist. Young was represented in his second appeal effort by a new barrister, Jim Sturman QC, known for his work revealing miscarriages of justice such as the cases of Colin Stagg, entrapped by an undercover police officer who answered his lonely-hearts ad into a false confession of the murder of Rachel Nickel on Wimbledon Common in 1992, and Mark Dallagher, falsely implicated by unreliable ear print evidence for a 1996 murder. His junior in Young's second appeal, Allison Pople, would go on to represent Andy Coulson, the penultimate editor of the *News of the World* and a senior staffer for Prime Minister David Cameron, when he was prosecuted and imprisoned over the tabloid's phone-hacking scandal. Young himself was also an advocate in his own case, penning his own lengthy appeal ground that his lawyers disowned, but which a judge bafflingly granted him leave to argue. Although the appeal ground apparently complained bitterly of Young's trial representation, Pople assured a concerned Court of Appeal that there was no plan to call Young's former barrister David Penry-Davey, now a High Court judge, as a witness.

In May 2002, seven-and-a-half years after Young's second trial, Sturman asked for the Court of Appeal's help in obtaining possible evidence relevant to the appeal. The list of requests was lengthy: a fresh statement from Gilchrist (who had been referring queries to his own solicitor, which was also his new firm, who in turn said that Young's former lawyer could not remember many of the details sought); the originals of the various recordings of phone calls in the case (so they could be examined by a new forensic audiology expert, Dr Peter French); the audio of part of Mr Justice Blofeld's direction to the jury (which Young claimed was not properly transcribed); and more legal aid to cover additional investigations. Eighteen months later, Pople was back in court seeking more: a report by the Sussex police about Gilchrist (apparently about the allegations made against him by his other disgruntled client, Colin Waters); a copy of Young's financial statements (for review by his former business solicitor); more money for a forensic examination of the phone recording tapes by Dr French; a written statement from Stephen Holt, Penry-Davey's junior at Young's trial and a future Circuit Court judge (about the contested alibi statement); and copies of the log of the Lloyds Bank's CCTV.

Pople also convinced the Court of Appeal to make the following order:

> A subpoena will be served, through the prosecution, on Norman Duncan, within 21 days requiring him, first, within 14 days, to deliver to the Court either both the tape of conversation between police officers relating to evidence in the appellant's case and the tape of conversation with Roger Lee…

The alleged tapes' alleged contents were explosive. They supposedly recorded the Sussex police admitting to tampering with the evidence against Young and Roger Lee admitting to killing the Fullers. Five years earlier, Lee (or, at least, someone with the same name who lived in the same caravan park as Lee did in 1994) was charged with a different murder: that of George Ennis, a 40-year old, tall with dreadlocks, who died of head injuries after being beaten in a memorial garden in the Kent village of Aylesford. Ennis's *de facto* spouse was Lee's aunt and Lee was cousin to her three teenage children. He was arrested along with his mother, the *de facto* spouse's sister. Although Lee's case quickly reached the courts as a test case for recently introduced criminal discovery procedures, there is no published record of any trial or conviction resulting.

The source of the alleged tape, Norman Duncan (who told journalists and Young's former solicitors 'over a pint' that he had the tapes of the police's and Lee's alleged admissions) was much better known to England's courts. He had been a key witness in a disastrous prosecution a decade earlier of three men for a series of violent crimes near London's ring road, the M25. When it belatedly emerged that Duncan was a police informant who received a hefty reward for his assistance and was never prosecuted for his admitted theft of a car said to be used in the crimes, the European Court of Human Rights ruled that the defendants' trial was unfair. The Court of Appeal (including Blofeld, Young's judge in his re-trial) reversed an earlier ruling by the same court (including Lord Taylor), adding the 'M25 Three' to the list of English miscarriages of justice.

In 2003, the Court of Appeal was understandably disturbed by the plethora of requests in Young's case and the time further investigations would take:

THE VICE PRESIDENT: We have in mind of course this conviction was in 1994.

MISS POPLE: My Lord, absolutely.

THE VICE PRESIDENT: At the moment, I do not say this in a critical sense, everything is open-ended as to when this appeal might ultimately see the light of day.

MISS POPLE: We are acutely conscious of that my Lord.

But it was another year before the court heard Young's new appeal. By then, it was clear that the defence would not be making any submissions about Dr French's fresh analysis of the phone recordings or Norman Duncan's supposed tapes. Rather, the main fresh evidence concerned the two schoolgirls (discussed in *Chapter 6*) who said they may have seen two people burst from Blackmans Cottage around the time the Fullers were killed. At Young's trials, the prosecution had suggested that the pair were thinking of another morning, but Young's new lawyers had since arranged for the one of them, now in her 20s, to be shown enhanced stills from the Lloyds Bank CCTV. In May 2004, she told the defence that she thought she was visible in a still at 9.05 am on 10th February 1993, but she later retracted that claim by email and maintained her doubts about whether she had seen both men she described on the same day. Unsurprisingly, the Court of Appeal thought the new evidence made no difference.

The appeal judges were similarly dismissive of a lacklustre list of complaints about how various pieces of evidence were dealt with at Young's re-trial in the Old Bailey. Was Young's alibi notice prepared incompetently? No, as Young himself characterised it as 'carefully non-committal'. Should the defence have used a phone record to confirm Young's account of the timing of his conversation with insurance representative Martin Bell? Probably, but no-one at the trial seemed to think the timing was important. Did Mr Justice Blofeld err in inexplicably adding the fictitious words 'the back garden is clear' to his description of the recorded conversation between Young and Harry? Yes, but the jury had a correct transcript before them. Did Blofeld confuse the jurors when he discussed a key found at Young's house that fitted either Blackmans Cottage or the door of Young's cousin's house? Yes, but he also correctly told the jury that the key didn't prove anything. Should the defence have told the jury that alternative suspect Colin Gabriel admitted that he was keeping an eye out for Harry on the day the dealer was killed? Maybe, but that paled beside other evidence implicating Gabriel. These mild confusions and Monday-night quarterbacking are the stuff of complex circumstantial evidence appeals.

But Young's point was that his case was always a close one because of Harry's many enemies. So, even minor errors, whether in his solicitor's office, the courtroom or jury room, may have converted a slightly-too-weak case into a wrongful conviction, especially in combination. The Court of Appeal's response, in December 2004, was short:

> But the fact is that at the end of the day it is clear that whoever entered the house and killed Mr and Mrs Fuller is likely to have done so by invitation and therefore to have been a friend, not an enemy, or perceived as such. It stretches coincidence too far to find that the appellant, who fits that category, was there at the time, went into the house, had had the gun which was used to shoot the Fullers, had identical bullets in his home and had substantial debts which were alleviated by a payment of £6,000 in cash the day after was not that person.

Ten years after he was convicted a second time, Young's legal case was over.

A lighter tale

> We have heard barristers talking about the 'Ouija board case' which this has now become.

The 'Ouija board case' label — previously attached to the American cases on taxation and séance-inspired murders described in *Chapter 3* — has been claimed by Young's case since 1994, very likely permanently. Alongside an article noting the Johnsons' dislike of the case's new nickname, the media reported a final exchange between the prosecution and the Lord Chief Justice in Young's first appeal:

> Crown counsel Mr Michael Lawson, QC, had contended that the court could open the way to the eventual abolition of the jury system by quashing Young's convictions on the basis of what had happened at the hotel. Lord

Taylor refuted 'such a fearful spectre' and said that what happened in the case was unique.

The case was indeed unique, and remains so.

In 1997, the *Weekly World News* published a report of another such case from Germany, this time fitting the hypothetical described by Professor John Spencer (*Chapter 5*) and later considered by the House of Lords:

> Jury member Ada Bauer said the jury was hopelessly deadlocked when one of them proposed using the Ouija board. 'Judge Schlendt doesn't understand how bad it was getting in that juror room' she said. 'We were screaming at one another and no-one would give in.'…Mrs. Bauer said before the Ouija board was used there was a strict agreement reached among the jurors. 'We all said we'd go along with whatever the Ouija board revealed', she added.

Alas, the sometimes suspect *Weekly World News* was the only paper to report this startling incident, with no other media source covering the murders supposedly at issue, the defendant 'Peter Giradet', the murder trial in Dortmund or even the existence of an English-style jury system in contemporary Germany (The last German jurors sat during the Weimar Republic).

In lay settings, the Ouija board case lives on as a punchline about the jury system, a regular bullet point in internet clickbait lists of the world's dumbest jurors or the like. In one of the better lists, describing 'five stupid juries', *The Old Ship* jurors appropriately appear alongside the Colorado jurors who discussed a hotel room Bible while deliberating on the death penalty (described in *Chapter 3*). But the four jurors also share the billing with lone jurors who did quite different (and much more egregious) things—Gillian Guess, the British Columbian juror who slept with one of the defendants during the trial and served prison time for her deeds (discussed in *Chapter 1*) and a New Zealand juror who confessed to his horrified colleagues that he was constantly aroused during a child sexual abuse trial. The list is rounded out by a much more minor sin: some Australian jurors who were caught playing Sudoku in the jury box during a lengthy (and, it was said, extremely dull) drug trafficking trial.

Describing all of these instances as 'stupid' lumps together a number of very different threats to the jury system. As well, in my view, the evidence addressed in *Chapter 6* of this book should put to rest any suggestions that the particular problem raised by Young's case was the jurors' intelligence.

In legal settings, beyond its afterlife as a precedent and later punch-bag in the debate over jury confidentiality, the Ouija board case persists as a recurrent teachable moment. One of the best treatments is by Professor Gary Slapper, who is one of the few academics other than Spencer to engage with the case's challenges. Slapper uses the Ouija board case in his book *How the Law Works* as one of a number of illustrative tales in a chapter about jurors. He rightly discusses it, without pejoratives, alongside the Bristol jury that wanted to tap the expertise of one of their number who was a tyre specialist and the Newcastle juror who asked for the defendant's birth date (both described in *Chapter 3*) Slapper also details cases of jurors who refuse to convict against the evidence on political or emotional grounds (what is known as 'jury nullification') and more mundane juror indiscretions that pose mild practical quandaries for courts: a foreman in a jewel robbery trial who accidentally handcuffed himself with an exhibit while in the jury room, another who disastrously coughed during the word 'not' in the foreman's verdict of acquittal, and two jurors who nearly came to blows after an argument about smoking. While all of these cases are reasonably well-documented, the final case he describes is quite different:

> The tale concerns an indecency case. A woman witness was giving evidence and was asked what the man in the dock had said to her. She was too embarrassed to repeat it in open court, so the judge asked her to write it down. She did, and what she wrote was 'Would you care for a screw?' This document was passed around the jury until it reached juror number 12, an elderly gentleman who was fast asleep. Sitting next to him was a fairly personable young lady. She read the note, nudged her neighbour and, when he was awake, handed it to him. He woke with a start, read it and, with apparent satisfaction, folded it and put it carefully away in his wallet. When the judge said, 'Let that be handed up to me', the juryman shook his head and replied, 'It's purely a private matter, my Lord'.

The legal issues posed by this incident, which Slapper attributes to barrister-turned-*Rumpole of the Bailey* author John Mortimer QC, go unexplored. Alas, what Slapper describes as 'a good example of a lighter tale' is simply too perfect to be true. Internet debunker *Snopes* points out that a version of the story appeared in the very first episode of *Saturday Night Live* in 1975 (credited to George Carlin, with George Coe, Chevy Chase and Jane Curtin as judge, prosecutor and witness, and John Belushi and Gina Radner as, respectively, the nudging and dozing jurors—the genders are reversed from Mortimer's version).

The likewise too-perfect (but nevertheless well-evidenced) Ouija board case also has its doubters or distorters in legal settings. New Zealand judges reportedly speak of jurors who were 'said to' have used a Ouija board. In 2007, the New South Wales Court of Criminal Appeal, perhaps aware of Professor Spencer's criticisms of English law, got the result wrong:

> The prohibition against admitting evidence of the jury's deliberations is such that the English Court of Appeal refused to set aside a verdict that had been arrived at after three members of the jury consulted (and were apparently influenced by) a ouija board.

Such mistakes are partly explained by a quirk of contemporary online legal sources—while most modern judgements from the English Court of Appeal are a simple search away on public judgement repositories such as the British and Irish Legal Information Institute, *R v Young* remains locked behind commercial paywalls and inside dusty law libraries. As mentioned in this book's Foreword, a more lamentable recent trend is that judicial discussions of the case have shifted from doubt or amusement to anger, accusing the jurors of improper conduct, misconduct akin to lechery, 'irresponsible behaviour' (in Australia's High Court) or (England's Court of Appeal in 2010) 'the most egregious abuse of the jury's oath'. These harsh descriptions seem to have in mind Lord Steyn's hypothetical about the use of the Ouija board in the jury room, rather than the actual events in *The Old Ship*.

Such a stupid thing

> The situation has left us with a very jaundiced view of British justice.

England's justice system stumbled, but did not fall. The case exposed the jury system's potential weaknesses in a very embarrassing way. Nevertheless, the system got the right result, at the end of the day and throughout. Murderer Stephen Young was convicted, given a new trial, convicted again and had his conviction affirmed. That's the official verdict on the Ouija board case. But it's not my view. I don't think the system got the case right, at the end of the day or throughout.

What exactly happened at *The Old Ship*? While the basics of the four jurors' use of the makeshift Ouija board isn't in doubt, the difficult question is whether any of Adrian's jury were influenced by Harry Fuller's supposed answers at the séance. The Court of Appeal in 1994 allowed Young's appeal because it thought that the sequence of events supported that possibility, despite the jurors' own denials:

> The three women jurors were upset about what emerged. One was crying and took the view that it had gone too far. Why, if it was just a game? And why, when the verdict had been unanimous, should one juror (not one of the four) have been sufficiently concerned to consult a solicitor and make a statement about what had happened?

The Court of Appeal posed these two questions rhetorically, but this book suggests alternative answers to the ones the judges had in mind. The contents of the 999 recording and David's remarks on the *Modern Times* documentary, discussed in *Chapter 6*, provide an all too plausible explanation for the three jurors' tears: the purported communication with one of the Fullers, perhaps initiated in response to the emotional burden of knowing Nicola's fate, may well have left the more empathetic of the hotel room jurors as overwhelmed as David's jury was. As for Adrian's motivations as whistleblower, there is no reason to doubt that he was worried about what he was told had happened in *The Old Ship*. But he also may have had (or at least acquired) a different motivation to speak out, in the form of a cash payment by the tabloid to an unemployed man.

Given the inherent unlikelihood of jurors' believing that they were actually speaking to a murder victim with a glass and pieces of paper, these alternative assessments of the evidence suggest a more likely take on the Ouija board incident: that it was exactly what the jurors themselves claimed it was: a mere drunken game, albeit one that was likely more melancholic than raucous. We can never be certain about any of that, and even the jurors themselves may not know. It is possible that some light may be shed by Adrian's handwritten letter, or the 15 affidavits the Court of Appeal obtained (from the 12 jurors, two bailiffs, and the solicitor Adrian first spoke to), but those have never been released, at least partly because of the (likely unintended) ten-year order prohibiting their publication. If they are still in the court file, they are now governed by England's general rule barring the release of unpublished government documents until 30 years after their creation (that is, July 2024).

Many will argue that the Court of Appeal was still right to overturn Young's original conviction because of the mere chance that the jurors took the Ouija board seriously, or alternatively because of the mere facts that four jurors separated themselves from the rest and that some of Young's jury were drunk, disobedient and secretive the night before they changed his life. These are indeed worrying matters, but they need to be weighed against the costs of the re-trial, costs that were born by the taxpayer, the lawyers, the witnesses, David's jury and the victims' families. It is these costs (rather than jury secrecy rules) that explain why most claims about jury conduct do not result in a re-trial. As described in *Chapter 5*, the Court of Appeal heard dozens of appeals involving alleged juror misconduct in 1994 alone, but only allowed two of them. It is possible that, but for Adrian's story being published first in the *News of the World* and attracting widespread attention and disdain, the Court of Appeal might have been similarly inclined to dismiss Young's appeal as founded on unrealistic assumptions about how 12 adults would resolve a complex, horrific case, assumptions that all involved had denied.

Even putting to one side the costs of the re-trial, the Court of Appeal's conclusion meant that the judges and commentators drew a single meagre lesson from the incident: that jurors can be extraordinarily stupid and irresponsible and need to be forced to do their job without emotion or distraction and punished if they don't. After Young's re-trial, one of the victim's relatives called for the Ouija board jurors to be prosecuted:

> Mr Fuller's brother Tom, 39, said: 'The jurors that used the Ouija board should be brought to justice themselves for the double anguish they have caused us by doing such a stupid thing.'

He added: 'We all went through months' more agony because of them'. Tom Fuller's call wasn't heeded, but his stance eventually took hold in response to a different 'stupid thing' that jurors were said to be wont to do in subsequent decades

In 2015, the UK parliament enacted several new offences intended to respond to the threat the internet posed to the jury system. One offence, responding to jurors who Googled aspects of the evidence (and potentially uncovered inadmissible information) barred jurors from researching their case. A new section 20A Juries Act 1974 was inserted by the Criminal Justice and Courts Act 2015 under which:

(2) A person researches a case if (and only if) the person—

    (a) intentionally seeks information, and

    (b) when doing so, knows or ought reasonably to know that the information is or may be relevant to the case.

(3) The ways in which a person may seek information include—

    (a) asking a question,

    (b) searching an electronic database, including by means of the internet,

    (c) visiting or inspecting a place or object,

>   (d)   conducting an experiment, and
>
>   (e)   asking another person to seek the information.

While very few people would describe a séance as research, some of these terms in the statute—'seeks information', 'asking a question', 'conducting an experiment'—plausibly cover the use of a makeshift Ouija board to question a person connected with a trial, as the jurors in Young's first trial did. The information sought (and obtained) is quite dubious of course, but the same is true of much information online.

As well, England now has a second offence for other jury misbehaviour, hastily added to the same statute after a new internet threat emerged: social media. In 2012, juror Kasim Davey (young and unemployed, like Adrian), who was empanelled in a child sexual assault trial, used his phone to post on Facebook on the bus ride home: 'Woooow I wasn't expecting to be in a jury Deciding a paedophile's fate, I've always wanted to Fuck up a paedophile & now I'm within the law!' After one of his 400 'friends' alerted the court, Davey was dismissed from the jury and later prosecuted for contempt of court. The High Court rejected his arguments that the post was just to make him seem exciting to his friends, that he was diligent in his duties and that he was unaware that what he did was forbidden. He was sentenced to two months in prison. In response, the UK Parliament added a further offence to the Statute Book (the new section 20C(2) Juries Act 1974) covering the following behaviour:

> 'Prohibited conduct' means conduct from which it may reasonably be concluded that the person intends to try the issue otherwise than on the basis of the evidence presented in the proceedings on the issue.

Had the events of Tuesday 22nd March 1994 occurred in England today, there would be a good argument that all four jurors would have committed this offence. By that token, the same would also be potentially true of jurors who read Bibles, ask for a defendant's date-of-birth, nod at members of the public gallery, smile or grimace at a party, complain about the length of a trial, make racist remarks, write love letters to barristers or rely on the knowledge of a tyre expert in the jury room. Likewise, jurors who use contemporary social media as a means of coping with the stresses of their role now risk not only the derision heaped onto the Ouija board jurors, but also time in prison.

Jekyll and Hyde

> We have even considered not staying in a country with a system like this. Where's the sense in it all?

Nicola Fuller's grieving parents faced a further burden: sharing a town with the family of the man convicted of their daughter's murder. Their difficulties were alluded to by a letter to the editor of the *Kent and Sussex Courier* from a Tunbridge Wells resident a week after the conclusion of the first trial:

> If a great friend is convicted of murder (report, March 25) and you feel sure he was not guilty, whom dare you blame for what you see as a great mistake? Not the family of the murder victim, please. They were certainly neither the judge nor the prosecuting counsel. And they were not members of the jury. Nor did they give evidence in the crown court. They sat in the public gallery hearing the horrifying evidence given by several witnesses. I suggest that anyone who says or implies that the family are in any way to blame owes them an apology.

Michael Johnson, who was 'born and bred just a few miles from Pembury', told the media:

> We are disgusted. We have been shunned. Apart from our friends and neighbours, who have been very good, we have had almost no support from the village at all. I have even been stopped in the street and asked if I have got the right person. He had such a high profile in the village. The thing is,

when you get these really evil people they do appear normal. It is part of the act. How wrong can people be?

For my part, I am sure that the police, prosecution and (both) juries 'got the right person'. But I am not at all sure that the English courts uncovered the entire truth of what happened at Blackmans Cottage that Wednesday morning in February 1993.

The defence's theory—that the Fullers' killer had nothing to do with Stephen Young—is not plausible. It's true that Harry had many much more plausible enemies than his insurance broker. But, Young's connections to the Fullers' deaths—his presence, his gun, his debts—are far too many to be a coincidence, and Young's business relationship with Harry gave him an important advantage over Harry's enemies when it came to opening the door to Blackmans Cottage. But the prosecution's theory—that imminent bankruptcy and exposure of dishonesty drove a well-liked village insurance broker with a loving family to brutally slay a married couple in the hope of obtaining some quick cash—has never struck me as satisfactory. Young's circumstances, while dire, are all too common, but cold-blooded killings for that reason alone are very rare, at least for adults with no history of violence or disturbance.

The police investigation's longest serving head, Detective Chief Superintendent Graham Hill, was well aware of these problems in the prosecution case. After Young's second conviction, he told the media his theory that the broker:

> …has a split personality. On one hand he is quite clearly, in the eyes of those who know him, a well thought-of family man. But there is a callous, cold-blooded dark side which made him commit these terrible murders. All the indications show that having killed Harry and Nicola, he remained cool and in control with no sign of panic. That is the way he has acted ever since. He has shown no sign of having this on his conscience. He was relaxed during questioning, never flustered and appeared confident his lies could explain away every item of evidence.

The *Evening Standard* labelled this Young's 'Jekyll and Hyde existence'. After Young was convicted a second time, Hill left his detective role to join a charitable victim support service in West Sussex that gave emotional and practical help to victims and court witnesses, perhaps influenced by his stark take on the pure evil hidden within an insurance broker. But, while Hill's 'split personality' theory is compatible with the available evidence, there's nothing to support it other than it being the only way to explain the stance that the prosecution took at both of Young's trials.

There is, however, a different theory about two personalities that not only explains both the prosecution and the defence evidence, but is positively supported by evidence obtained both before and after Young's trials. That theory is that two or more people, including Young, were responsible for the Fullers' deaths. What if Young worked together with one of Harry's real enemies? Perhaps someone who wanted Harry dead and asked (or dragooned) Young into participating, because Young could supply a weapon, needed money, was trusted by the car dealer and (but for the Geemarc answering machine tape) would not be on the police's radar. Or perhaps Young's financial needs drove him into the criminal milieu that surrounded Harry, ultimately pairing him with someone who had more designs on Harry than his wads of cash. Importantly, these scenarios—or any number of variations—are positively supported by the evidence at Young's trials.

The basics are straightforward. Everyone accepts that Harry had plenty of enemies, notably those who (with reason) thought the car dealer was a grass. And a scenario in which Young was working with someone more violent—with Young's role limited to setting up the encounter and (perhaps) acting as a sentinel—fits not just with Young's known movements that Wednesday morning, but also much of the various stories he provided to the police and the courts, including the phone calls, the sight (and perhaps the shock) of Harry's corpse, and the various threats to his family. The involvement of Young and one other even fits with the oddity that, although Harry was thought to have been keeping at least £13,000 in cash in Blackmans Cottage, the broker only paid off £6,300 of his many debts.

What is more, the two person theory is well-supported by other evidence pointing to the involvement of more than one person in the Fullers' deaths, including the accounts of witnesses set out in the *Crimewatch* reconstruction, the statements of the schoolgirls and evidence obtained after Young lost his second appeal. Since 2004, Young has been represented by a new barrister, Simon McKay, who is pursuing a further review of his conviction by the Criminal Cases Review Commission, the body set up in 1995 as a back-stop against English miscarriages of justice. The centrepiece of McKay's application is a new analysis of the 999 recording by an American forensic audiologist, Stuart Allen. Allen's report states:

> The footsteps observed at 00:02:24 were most likely created by an unsub [unknown subject] wearing hard soled shoes walking on a hard floor and carpeting. In addition to the sounds of footsteps, what appears to be whispering, presumably to another unsub present in the room, are also barely audible. A set of footsteps dissimilar to that belonging to unsub#1 can also be heard in the background noise level. The footsteps made by unsub#2 were most likely created by the unsub wearing soft or rubber soled shoes whilst walking on a hard floor and carpeting. Although the whispers are mostly unintelligible the word 'here' can be heard. Additional unintelligible whispering accompanied by two sets of footsteps are audible when the unsubs (2) are heard leaving through a door with a spring assisted closure attached.

In short, Allen heard (at least) two people walking around Blackmans Cottage after Nicola's death, one with hard shoes, one with soft ones, and whispering. When it rejected McKay's application for a review, the commission expressly relied on the two person theory of Young's guilt. While Young has good reason to be aggrieved that the commission relied on a scenario the prosecution never suggested at his trials to decline to investigate his convictions further, everyone else with a stake in the trial should be troubled by Allen's opinion (if correct) for a different reason. Not only does it mean that justice has been partly denied to the Fullers, but that at least one killer—perhaps the actual shooter of the newlyweds —might still be at large.

The pain is still here

> But it isn't that—it's about justice for our daughter and letting the truth be known.

Feeling unsupported by their neighbours in Pembury, the Johnsons found solace in victims' groups, especially one founded by Mark Manwaring, whose father and sister were killed a year before the Fullers. Barbara told the media:

> Mark has been absolutely super, a wonderful friend and a great comfort to us. We thought we were going round the bend at times but he told us 'That's normal—it's exactly what happened to me'. We just didn't know how stable our thoughts were, we couldn't assess our emotions. We have decided to join the group Parents of Murdered Children and hope we can use our experience to help others.

Norman Brennan, a serving police officer who founded the Victims of Crime Trust in 1994, attended both trials. In 2004, he commented:

> There is never a nice murder but the crime Stephen Young committed was one of the most appalling, premeditated double murders I have ever heard about.

He added that he had no doubt that the trials had an impact on the health of the Fullers' relatives. Tom, Harry's brother, said after the re-trial:

> Stephen Young is an animal who should be put down. I would like to see hanging brought back for people like him. You can hardly explain what it has been like for both families to go through this ordeal. It's like someone having their hand in your guts and slowly pulling them out.

The Johnsons have both suffered health setbacks since the trials. Barbara had a heart attack in 1999, while Michael had a stroke the following year. Each were only in their mid-50s.

Crimes have long-lasting and cascading consequences. The responsibility of the killer (or killers) of Harry and Nicola Fuller for the pain felt by the Johnsons, and much more besides, is clear. Harry's family has generally maintained a media silence, but the Johnsons have repeatedly detailed their family's grief. Barbara told *Crimewatch*: 'I feel that there is part of me that's just gone and there's this big hole that will never be filled.' As the first trial approached, they hung a floral tribute from the tree outside Blackmans Cottage:

> Dear Nicky, It is now a year since you were taken from us but the pain is still here until we meet again. God has you in his keeping. We love you in all our hearts. Love from Mum, Dad, Michelle and Sebastien.

Following their shock watching *Songs of Praise*, Michael explained:

> My wife feels very lonely without her and my daughter Michelle cannot accept she has lost not only her sister, but her best friend. Nicky was such a presence. We spoke to her on the phone every day.

Barbara later revealed that Nicola's younger sister commenced counselling a decade after the murders:

> I don't think Michelle really grieved, she was too busy looking after us. Last year, she heard about the appeal and went to pieces.

The stories of David and the 999 operator described in Chapter Six make it clear that at least some others also suffered serious psychological harm because of the events of February 10th 1993. Any number of professionals and officials, as well as 36 jurors, had to listen to the recording of Nicola's final phone call. Without minimising the blame rightly imposed on the criminal or criminals, some of these people—notably David's jury—only bore that burden because of events in *The Old Ship* and the Court of Appeal in 1994.

Did the Fullers' callous slaying have a further consequence: lasting harm to the entire institution of trial by jury? Writing on the day after the Court of Appeal's 1994 decision was announced, senior lecturer (later Professor) Gary Slapper observed:

> There are those who believe that if ever jury secrecy was abandoned here, trial by jury would eventually go the same way.

So far, Lord Taylor's rejection of 'such a fearful spectre' has proven correct. Indeed, as this book was being finished, Lady Justice Hallet, despite repeating the Ouija board tale (more accurately than most) in the 35th Blackstone lecture, concluded:

> I accept too much depends on anecdote. Too much depends on prejudice—the examples I have given of jury misconduct or alleged incompetence are a mere handful compared to the many thousands of jury trials that take place every year.

Still, I have no doubt that, if jury trials are ever abolished or significantly constricted, an anecdote about the events of March 22nd 1994 will form part of the institution's obituary.

In this book, I've argued that much of the criticism that has flowed from the Ouija board case to the wider jury system is due to the repeated misdescriptions of the case throughout as suggesting that the whole jury used an actual Ouija board to reach its verdict. There was no jury in the hotel room (just four jurors) and scarcely any board. More importantly, not only did the Court of Appeal not decide that any of the jurors had used the results of a séance in to determine his or her verdict, but there is every reason to accept the four jurors' claim that the events at *The Old Ship* had no effect on the verdict at all. While I don't think that exonerates those four jurors from some responsibility for the damage their actions in the hotel room caused, I think that blame is shared by many others, including Adrian, the defence's lawyers, the editors, authors and publishers at the *News of the World,* the Court of Appeal (including the Lord Chief Justice, Peter Taylor) and Professor John Spencer and others who have made use of the case.

The great pity is that all of this outrage, hysteria and even humour—not to mention the legal and political manoeuvres that have followed—have come at the expense of recognising a different threat to the jury system that the case truly exemplifies. The circumstances of the four Ouija board jurors bear close consideration. There is every reason to think that they (and their eight colleagues) were just as distressed as David's jury was by the evidence about Nicola's death. They also faced the burden of having their private behaviour (and possible turmoil) outed and scorned by a tabloid, investigated by a police officer, condemned by multiple courts and pilloried by a host of lay, legal and academic commentators. The Court of Appeal's judgement accused them (on doubtful evidence) of believing in ghosts, annulled the result of their five weeks of service and laid the blame on them for the many costs of the re-trial. The Contempt of Court Act 1981 continues to largely bar them from explaining their actions. While nothing can come close to the traumas that the Fullers' deaths imposed on their families, the Ouija board case is also a potent lesson on the traumas the jury system itself can cause and the dangers of not taking steps to manage the stresses of the juror role.

Nicola's father rightly equates justice for his daughter with 'letting the truth be known'. My view is that, at least once the door to *The Old Ship* hotel room was opened wide, first by a tabloid and then by a court, the only way to achieve justice in this case was to let the truth be known about what happened behind it. The whole truth.

Whatever the merits of jury secrecy, there is no excuse for limiting ourselves to arid legal argument, mock horror and amusing anecdotes on those occasions when we lift the veil. Rather, we should seek to understand what that jury experienced, including learning about the task they were required to undertake, the evidence they were made to consider and the effect those things had on them and others. Not only should we be prepared to approach their seemingly outlandish behaviour with sympathy but we should always ask: what might we have done if we had to bear their burden?

If that stance had been taken from the outset when it came to the Ouija Board case, then the tale would I believe have prompted small but important changes to how we assist jurors in their role. Such a positive outcome, amidst the horrors that occurred on 10th February 1993, might even have brought a small measure of solace to Stephen Young's many victims.

The Ouija Board Jurors

Afterword

Formal sources

There are many living people who were involved in the Ouija board case, either personally, or as investigators, or in the legal proceedings. These likely include most of the jurors (only one of whom has been publicly identified), Stephen Young, the families of Harry and Nicola, the various lawyers and investigators, and many other witnesses. I have not tried to interview any of these people. I am an academic, not a journalist, and lack the expertise to locate people who do not have public profiles, propose, arrange and conduct interviews (especially with people traumatised by crime) or to meet journalistic ethical standards (such as giving people opportunities to respond to claims made by others).

I also suspect that most of these people would not want to speak to me about the case, either for professional reasons or personal ones, especially as my agenda as an academic differs from the understandable interests of those closely involved. Indeed, because Young is continuing to pursue avenues for establishing his innocence, I doubt that the parties in the legal proceedings would be willing to speak with me or make non-public documents available. I am conscious that not pursuing these sources may deny me insights or corrections of errors. That is one reason why I have made an effort throughout this book to give voice to everyone I can by highlighting what they have reportedly said on the public record, including in the running quotes throughout each chapter.

This book is instead mainly sourced from two sets of publicly available documents. The first is the available court record. There are two formal judgements on the case: *R v Young (Stephen)* [1995] 2 WLR 430; QB 324; 2 Cr. App 379 (the judgement allowing Young's first appeal) and *R v Stephen Young* [2004] EWCA Crim 3520 (the judgement dismissing Young's second appeal). Neither is available on free online services (like Bailli). Instead, I used *Justis*, a commercial service. As a bonus, that service also holds transcripts of half a dozen or so procedural hearings in the two appeals (which can be found by searching for 'Stephen Andrew Young').

The second source is available media articles. I am particularly grateful to the Wadhurst History Society, which keeps a scrapbook of local media articles (and some photos and public documents) on the Fuller case and allowed me to examine and copy it. I supplemented those articles with ones kept on microfilm at the Tunbridge Wells Library's local studies collection (which includes some different editions of local papers to the Wadhurst ones) and, especially for articles after the Ouija board revelation, a commercial database of national and international newspapers, *Factiva* (searching for the victims' names or 'ouija').

Both of these sources are publicly accessible (albeit sometimes for a fee, or only in a particular location). The same is true for nearly every other source for this book (the only exception is one source I used in *Chapter 7*). Some potentially very useful sources of information about the case are not publicly available at the moment:

- The unsigned letter from the juror and the 15 affidavits taken by the Treasury Solicitor from the 12 jurors, two bailiffs and Young's solicitor, used by the Court of Appeal in 1994. While Taylor LCJ's orders make it clear that he intended these to eventually be accessible to the media (albeit with the jurors' names removed), this never happened (apart from the one affidavit partly set out in the court's judgement). The court file is now held by Her Majesty's Courts and Tribunals Service and is subject to the rule barring access for 30 years (presumably July 2024).
- Transcripts of the two trials and the substantive appeal hearings. Because these are generally discarded after five years, these transcripts are no longer publicly available.
- A *Crimewatch* episode originally broadcast on 17 September 1996 titled 'Iceman', which was apparently devoted to the Fuller case. Although this was publicly broadcast in England at least once, it is not now available in libraries or online. The

BBC will not release it to a member of the public without the express permission of the surviving victims.

In theory, I could have attended both trials in 1994 and the appeals hearings in 1994 and 2004, and watched 'Iceman' in 1996, but I didn't (having only started this book in 2014) and nor am I willing to I wait seven more years to (perhaps) see the affidavits and anything else in the 1994 appeal file.

Accordingly, this book represents an examination of all the publicly accessible sources I could locate that are available right now. A different, fuller or later examination may well cast a new light on the conclusions I've drawn or expose inaccuracies in the sources I've relied upon or the inferences I've drawn.

Particular sources used in single chapters, aside from the above, are briefly described below.

Foreword

The trial where a visitor in the public gallery was identified by an eye-witness as a war criminal was that of Ivan Polyukhovich in Adelaide in May 1993: see D Humphries, 'How Australia Became a Haven for War Criminals', *The Sydney Morning Herald*, 10th April 2010. The bank robbery trial where a conviction was overturned because the defendant was named 'Rob Banks' was also supposedly held in Adelaide, according to the *Weekly World News* of 3 May 1994, p. 39; alas, there is no record I could find of such a trial.

Lady Justice Hallett's 35th Blackstone Lecture is titled 'Trial by Jury — Past and Present' and is available at <https://www.judiciary.gov.uk/wp-content/uploads/2017/05/hallett-lj-blackstone-lecture-20170522-1.pdf>. The Australian High Court judgement referred to is *Smith v Western Australia* [2014] HCA 3.

Chapter 1: A Juror's Letter

The running quotes from juror Adrian are from G Jones, 'Booze, Dirty Jokes and then the Ouija Board', *News of the World*, 24th April 1994, pp

8-9. The quote from Lord Devlin is from P Devlin, *Trial by Jury* (Stevens & Sons, London, 1956), pp 41-43.

The judgements referred to are: *R v Kevin McCluskey* [1993] EWCA Crim J0 527-1 (juror received mobile phone call); *R v David Vincent Ward* [1994] EWCA Crim J0503-33 & [1995] EWCA Crim J0213-13 (juror allegedly nodded to victim's sister); *R v Mohammed Farooq & Mohammed Ramzan* [1994] EWCA Crim J0 510-22 (juror made calls from hotel); *R v David Terry Kerry* [1994] EWCA Crim J0725-19 & [1995] EWCA Crim J0302-6 (letter from regretful juror); *R v Henry & Clarkson* [1994] EWCA Crim J 1031-11 (anonymous letter alleging bribery); *R v Mohan Tharakan* [1994] EWCA Crim J1021-11 (jurors deliberated at hotel); *R v Guess*, 2000 BCCA 547; 148 CCC (3d) 321; 143 BCAC 51; [2000] CarswellBC 1971 & 2000 BCCA 602; 150 CCC (3d) 573; 147 BCAC 182 (juror slept with defendant); [2000] BCJ No 2023 (QL); 235 WAC 51 *Smith v Western Australia* [2014] HCA 3 & *Smith v The State of Western Australia [No 2]* [2016] WASCA 136 (anonymous note alleges assault of juror).

Sources on *The Old Ship*: R Flower, *The Old Ship: A Prospect of Brighton* (Croom Helm, England, 1986); Francis Hynes: *Hansard*, House of Commons, 17 August 1882 (Parliament—Privilege—Mr. Gray (Commitment of a Member of this House); David Penry-Davey: S Ward, 'Iron fist in a velvet glove to fight the bar's corner', *The Independent*, 14 February 1996 & 'Sir David Penry-Davey', *The Times*, 19 November 2015; Michael Lawson: M Lawson, 'A question of security?', 21 *The Circuiteer*, p8 & T Dutton, 'On the retirement of HH Judge Michael Lawson QC', 41 *The Circuiteer*, pp 6-7; Dorian Lovell-Pank: <http://www.6kbw.com/people/barristers/dorian-lovell-pank-qc>.

Chapter 2: Flash Harry

The running quotes from the juror's affidavit are from *R v Young (Stephen)* [1995] 2 WLR 430; QB 324; 2 Cr. App 379. The April 1993 episode of *Crimewatch* is available at <https://www.youtube.com/watch?v=XNQTC8UkF2w&t=1995s>.

Sources on Wadhurst: A Savidge & O Mason, *Wadhurst: Town of the High Weald* (2nd edition, 2014, Wadhurst History Society) & M Hart et al, *The Day Wadhurst Changed* (2006, Wadhurst History Society);

Pembury: D Miles, 'Councillors Comment', 73 *Pembury Village News*, p5; the Greenwoods: V Lorraine, 'Source of Evil', *Derby Evening Telegraph*, 27 January 2004; J Pennink, 'Gun deal duo face jail over murders', *Kent & Sussex Courier*, 30 January 2004; *R v Mitchell Verne Greenwood & William Mitchell Greenwood* [2005] EWCA Crim 2686.

Chapter 3: Only a Game

The running quotes (and other quotes from the Court of Appeal) are from *R v Young (Stephen)* [1995] 2 WLR 430; QB 324; 2 Cr. App 379. The quotes from Lord Taylor are from 'Judges told to dispel aloof image', *The Independent*, 15 April 1996; Hansard, House of Lords, 16 June 1992 (Second Reading Debate on Judicial Pensions and Retirement Bill). The 1886 article about Ouija boards is 'The New Planchette: A Mysterious Talking Board and Table Over Which Northern Ohio is Agitated', *New York Daily Tribune*, 28 March 1886, p8. The Op Ed by Gary Slapper is G Slapper, 'The dangers of spiritual guidance', *The Times*, 23 October 1994. The trial where a juror asked for the accused's birth date is described by P Wilkinson, 'Juror who wanted to find truth in stars', *The Times*, 9 July 1998. The quote from Mr Justice Waterhouse is in *R Waterhouse, Child of Another Century* (Radcliffe, London, 2013), p.259.

The other judgements referred to are: *Baltimore Talking Board Co Inc v Miles*, 280 F 658 (1922) & *White v Aronson*, [1937] USSC 154; 302 U.S. 16; 58 S.Ct. 95; 82 L.Ed. 20 (taxation of Ouija boards); *The City National Bank and Trust Company of Danbury, Executor*, 145 Conn. 518; 144 A.2d 338 (1958) & *Estate of Peck v Commissioner of Internal Revenue*, 40 T.C. 238 (1963) (Ouija board correspondent is will beneficiary); *State v DeMille*, 756 P.2d 81 (1988) (juror prays during child homicide trial); *R v Kevin McCluskey* [1993] EWCA Crim J0527-1 (juror received mobile phone call); *R v Clyde Frederick Charles Fricker* [1999] EWCA Crim J0624-2 (juror is a tyre specialist) *People v Harlan*, 109 P.3d 616 (2005) (jurors read bible during death penalty case).

Sources on Lesley Molseed: *R v Stefan Ivan Kiszko* (1979) 68 Cr. App R 62; J Rose et al, *Innocents: How Justice Failed Stefan Kiszko and Lesley Molseed* (Fourth Estate, London, 1997); *R v Ronald Castree* [2008] EWCA Crim 1866. Peter Taylor: J Morton, 'Obituary: Lord Taylor of

Gosforth', *The Independent*, 29 April 1997; 'Lord Taylor of Gosforth', *The Daily Telegraph*, 30 April 1997; G Robertson, 'Justice in all fairness', *The Guardian*, 30 April 1997; 'Lord Taylor of Gosforth', *The Times*, 30 April 1997. Ouija boards: <www.museumoftalkingboards.com>, L MacRobie, 'The strange and mysterious history of the Ouija board', *The Smithsonian*, 27 October 2013. Clothilde Marchand: D Krajicek, 'The Ouija board murder: tricking tribal healer Nancy Bowen to kill', *New York Daily News*, 21 March 2010.

Chapter 4: Iceman
The running quotes from Stephen Young are from 'Double murder suspect admits he lied to police', *The Kent and Sussex Courier* (Tunbridge Wells edition), 18 March 1994. The review of *Ali the Baddie* is 'Panto's slapstick fun', 73 *Pembury Village News* (available in the Pembury Library).

Chapter 5: Mansfield's Window
The running quotes are from J Spencer, 'Séances, and the Secrecy of the Jury-room' (1995) 54 *Cambridge Law Journal* 519. The YouTube video is at <https://www.youtube.com/watch?v=q8WzuDuXs80>. Spencer's other articles are 'Fraud by Anthony J. Arlidge, Jacques Parry: Review' (1986) 45 *Cambridge Law Journal* 332; 'Did the jury misbehave? Don't ask because we do not want to know' (2002) 61 *Cambridge Law Journal* 291; 'Juries: the freedom of act irresponsibly' (2004) *Cambridge Law Journal* 314.

The questions asked by the jurors in Vicky Pryce's trial are available at 'Vicky Pryce trial: 10 questions jury asked the judge', *The Guardian*, 21 February 2013. The column by Young's lawyer is S Gilchrist, 'Can we trust the jury?', *The Lawyer*, 19 July 1994, p9 (and the quote from Dickens is from *The Pickwick Papers*). The Australian case quoted is *R v Minarowska* (1995) 83 A Crim R 78, 86.

The judgements referred to are: *Hale v Cove* [1795] ER 1889 (jurors draw lots); *Vezey v Delaval*, *The Times*, 15 November 1785, p3 (see also *The Times*, 9 November 1785, p3; also reported as *Vaise v Delaval* [1785] ER 43) (jurors toss coin); *Owen v Warburton* [1805] ER 231 (jurors draw pencils); *Attorney General v New Statesman and Nation Publishing Co Ltd* [1981] QB 1 (article on jurors in Thorpe trial); *R v Tony James Godfrey &*

Colin Mark Harriman [1994] EWCA Crim J0701-12 (juror writes note to barrister); *R v Qureshi* [2001] EWCA Crim 1807; [2002] 1 WLR 518 (juror letter lists multiple complaints); *R v O'Connor; R v Mirza* [2004] 1 All ER 925 (jurors accused of racial bias).

The other claims of bizarre juror behaviour from 1994 are described in *R v Court* [1994] EWCA Crim J0509-9 (juror with a social engagement); *R v Parker* [1994] EWCA Crim J0609-29 (juror who giggled); *R v Kellard* [1994] EWCA Crim J0729-17 (juror who grimaced); *R v Holbrook* [1994] EWCA Crim J0912-3 (juror whose husband attended); *R v Dearden* [1994] EWCA Crim J1014-14 (juror who objected to obscene language); *R v Irvine* [1994] EWCA Crim J0609-7 (jury who mingled); R v Capon [1994] EWCA Crim J1031-12 (note alleging closed mind); *R v Walton* [1994] EWCA Crim J1110-6 (claim that juror knew defendant); *R v Kissi* [1994] EWCA Crim J1117-5 (dozing foreperson).

The two cases Spencer mentions on YouTube are described at I Hepburn, 'Sexy women jurors wreck a trial', *The Sun*, 31 October 1981, pp 1-2; and *R v Mears* [2011] EWCA Crim 2651. The collection of his works is J Spencer, *Noted But Not Invariably Approved* (Hart, Oxford, 2014). The quote from his colleague (Catherine Barnard) is at p.9.

Chapter 6: The Horrid Part

The running quotes from 'Dave' are from 'Jurors', *Modern Times* (BBC, 1997), produced by Nick Read, broadcast on BBC 2 on 16 April 1997 (and available at the British Library). The article about the documentary is M Driscoll, 'Jurors are sentenced for life too', *The Sunday Times*, 13 April 1997.

The judgements referred to are: *R v Paul Esslemont* [1994] EWCA Crim J0307-26 (distressing photo of toddler's injuries); *Heidt v Argani*, 214 P.3d 1255 (2009) (malpractice defendant assists distressed juror); *State v Ugalde*, 311 P.3d 772 (2013) (prosecutor channels child abuse victim); *Michael v The Chief Constable of South Wales Police* [2015] UKSC 2 (civil claim over 999 response).

Sources on Christopher French: 'Justice done—diary', *The Times*, 30 July 1996; R Borrill, 'Mr Justice French asked the barristers for help a day into his summing up', *The Irish Times*, 20 November 1996; Reynolds TD *v Times Newspapers Ltd & Ors* [1998] EWCA Civ 1172; J Bale, 'Reynolds wins retrial over judge's errors', *The Times*, 9 July 1998; 'Sir Christopher French', *The Daily Telegraph*, 27 March 2003; J Rozenberg, *Privacy and the Press* (Oxford UP, Oxford, 2004), p186. John Blofeld: *R v Taylor*, *Times Law Reports*, 15 June 1993; D Rose, 'Prisoner pursues claim of contact between judges', *The Observer*, 21 August 1994; A Luck, 'Meet the real Blofeld and Scaramanga', *Daily Mail*, 15 November 2015. Paul Esslemont: G Martin, 'The juror, a killer and the boy she thinks is innocent', *Evening Standard*, 3 June 1997; *R v Paul Esslemont* [1997] EWCA Crim J0704-16.

Chapter 7: Such a Fearful Spectre

The running quotes from Barbara and Michael Johnson are from M James, 'Our daughter's death is a joke', *The Courier*, 28 October 1994, p3. The quote from Lord Taylor about 'such a fearful spectre' appears on the same page.

The quote from Stuart Allen is the only non-public document I used as a source for this book. It is from a report supplied to me by barrister Simon McKay, who represented Stephen Young in his application to the Criminal Cases Review Commission. He supplied it to me at my request after I inquired about the status of Young's application. I am grateful to Mr McKay for making it available.

The interview with Phil Hall is in D Ponsford, 'From defending Fred Goodwin to Qatar: Former News of the World editor Phil Hall on ten years in PR', *Press Gazette*, 26 October 2015. The column by Young's lawyer is S Gilchrist, 'Can we trust the jury?', *The Lawyer*, 19 July 1994, p9. The anonymous article about Ouija boards is 'Things that go bump', *The Sunday Times*, 27 November 1994. The equally silly article about a German 'jury' using Ouija boards is A Morgan, 'Jury uses Ouija board to convict man of murder!', *Weekly World News*, 24 June 1997, p44. The list of 'stupid' juries is J Bennion et al, '5 stupid juries that prove the justice system is broken', *Cracked*, 18 July 2013. Professor Slapper's list is in G Slapper, *How the Law Works* (4th edition, Routledge, London, 2016), pp 200-215. The quote from Slapper is from G Slapper, 'The dangers of spiritual guidance', *The Times*, 23 October 1994. Lady Justice Hallett's 35th Blackstone Lecture is titled 'Trial by Jury—Past and Present' and is available at <https://www.judiciary.gov.uk/wp-content/uploads/2017/05/hallett-lj-blackstone-lecture-20170522-1.pdf>.

The judgements referred to are: *Attorney General v. Associated Newspapers Limited and Others* [1994] UKHL 1, [1994] 1 All ER 556 (article on jurors in Blue Arrow trial — the article is C Wolman, 'Common people common sense … common justice', *The Mail on Sunday*, 5 July 1992, pp 74-75); *Burrell v R* [2007] NSWCCA 65 (Australian judgement getting the result in Young wrong); *R v Burcombe* [2010] EWCA Crim 2818 ('most egregious abuse of the jury's oath'); *HM Attorney General v Davey* [2013] EWHC 2317 (Admin) (juror posts on Facebook); *Smith v Western Australia* [2014] HCA 3 ('irresponsible behaviour'). The statutory provisions are from the Criminal Justice and Courts Act 2015 (UK).

Sources on Gary Jones: <www.pressawards.org.uk>, *Ashworth Security Hospital v MGN Ltd* [2002] UKHL 29. Stephen Gilchrist: *R v The Legal Aid Board (Ex Parte Stephen Gilchrist)* [1994] EWCA Civ J0217-8; *R v Colin John Waters* [1995] EWCA Crim J1106-38; *In the Matter of Stephen Nigel Gilchrist v In the Matters of the Solicitors Act 1974* (Solicitors' Disciplinary Tribunal, No. 7775/1998, 2 June 1999); *In the Matter of a Solicitor v In the Matter of the Solicitors Act 1974* [1999] EWHC J1122-4; *In the Matter of Stephen Nigel Gilchrist v In the Matters of the Solicitors Act 1974* (Solicitors' Disciplinary Tribunal, No. 7914/1999, 25 February 2000); *Colin John Waters v R* [2006] EWCA Crim 139. George Ennis: J Bruce, 'Two quizzed over murder', *Kent Messenger*, 18 September 1998; *R (on the application of Lee) v Director of Public Prosecutions* [1999] EWHC Admin 242. Norman Duncan: *Rowe & Davis v UK* [2000] ECHR 91; *R v Davis & Ors* [2000] EWCA Crim 109.

Informal sources

Behind these formal sources are the book's many informal ones. The idea of writing a book on the Ouija board case came to me as I was walking from Wadhurst train station to Wadhurst's high street in mid-2016. I have three people in particular to thank for planting that idea in my mind. First, Jenny Morgan at Melbourne Law School for suggesting that I consider writing for a general audience after I voiced doubts about the continuing significance of academic publishing. Second, Paul Roberts of Nottingham Law School for his kind comment that my 2016 conference paper on the case recalled A B Simpson's *Cannibalism and the Common Law*. Third, the Wadhurst History Society, for its generous response to my walk-in request and for keeping a file on the case that left me sure that this story was worth telling at length.

I first wrote about the Ouija board case in passing as part of an online column, 'Divining the Jury', on 11 June 2013 on *Inside Story*, at <inside.com.au>, and later that year in the introduction to my evidence textbook co-authored with Andrew Palmer, *Uniform Evidence* (2nd edition, Oxford UP, Melbourne, 2014), Chapter 1. The next year, I examined the case in more detail at seminars at Melbourne Law School and the UNSW Faculty of Law and an address to the 2015 NSW Legal Aid Conference. In June 2016, I presented a draft paper on the case at a symposium on 'Commonsense Justice?' organized by Jill Hunter, Paul Roberts and Makoto Ibusuki and generously hosted by Oñati's *International Institute for the Sociology of Law*. I am very grateful for all of the invitations and feedback I received in these settings, particularly those of the IISL and Jill Hunter. Thanks also to Katy Barnett and Janina Jankowski for their extensive comments on drafts of this book.

Index

999 call/recording *135, 150, 185, 192*

A

absurdities *131*
Adrian *12, 69, 104, 119, 124, 133, 153, 185*
   letter from *200*
affidavits *23–26, 26, 32, 76, 116, 153, 186, 200*
alcohol *9, 20, 149, 166*
   drunken game *81*
alibi *59, 178, 180*
   notice of alibi *172*
Ali the Baddie *99–101*
Allen, Stuart *192*
ammunition/bullets *89–92, 103, 181*
anonymous calls *54, 103*
answering machine *58, 135*
   Boots machine *98*
   Geemarc machine *45, 86, 191*
Arrowhead (Operation Arrowhead) *94–105, 134*
astrology *77*
attainder *116*
Attorney-General *110*
audiology *148, 192*
Australia *182*
automatic writing *62*
automotism *65*
autopsy *52*

Aylesford *179*

B

babysitter *14*
bailiffs *69, 115, 186, 200*
balaclava *47*
Baltimore *63*
Bauer, Ada *182*
Bell, Martin *57, 180*
Bell, Sir Rodger *70*
Bernardo, Paul *154*
bias *139, 141*
   'apprehended bias' *130*
Bible *78, 80, 182*
Bingham, Lord Chief Justice *137*
Birmingham *18, 126*
Birmingham Six *59*
bizarre behaviour *126*
black-bonneted vehicle *96*
Blackmans Cottage *35, 56, 86, 142, 162, 190*
Blofeld, Mr Justice *138, 149*
blood *52*
   in cold blood *96*
Bloody Sunday *148*
Blue Arrow trial *164*
Bond, Elijah *63*
Booth, Det Insp Stuart *47*
booze *9, 156*

Bowen, Nancy 77
Brady, Ian 165
Brennan, Norman 193
Bridge, Lord 67
Bridge, Ralph 116
Brighton 10
    Brighton bombing 16
Brinklow, Harry 55, 57
Bristol 72
British Columbia 182
British Telecom 135, 142
Browning 9mm pistol 92
Buffalo 77
Bulger, James 44
bullets
    See ammunition; dum-dum bullets 59
burglary 96
Byron, Lord 16

C

call centre 146
Cambridge murder 124
Cameron, David 177
Canada 29
capital punishment 17, 193
    USA 78
Carr, Maxine 125
cartridge cases 144
cash 89, 94
    rolls/wads of cash 55
Castree, Ronald 83
CCTV 88, 103, 178, 180
Central London County Court 175
Charles II 16
Citizens Advice Bureau 13

class 62
Cluedo 65
coercion 32
Coller, Samantha 148
Colorado 78
common law 123
communication
    facilitated communication 65
    with the dead 71
confidentiality 183
conflict 30
Connecticut 71
constitutional headache 109
contamination 139
contempt of court 15, 21, 110, 188
    Contempt of Court Act 1981 109–111, 166
contract killing 95
Cordova, Jesus 79
corruption 18
cortège 50
costs 186
Coulson, Andy 177
Court of Appeal vii, 9, 12, 19, 22, 24, 65, 67, 85, 109, 167
    second appeal to 177
Court of Common Pleas 116
courtroom disclosures 169
Coventry 133
Crimewatch 44, 51, 83, 87, 96, 147, 192
Criminal Cases Review Commission 67, 192
Criminal Justice and Public Order Act 1994 86
Crowborough 37, 40

Crown Court *10*

D

Dahmer, Jeffrey *154*
Dallagher, Mark *177*
Davey, Kasim *188*
David *140, 149*
delusion *72*
DeMille, Tom *75*
detriment *80*
Devlin, Lord *17*
Dickens, Charles *16*
Dieu et mon droit *74*
Dilworth, Eve *148*
dirty jokes *20*
dishonesty *103*
distress *161*
divine oracles *74*
DNA *83*
Dortmund *182*
Dow, Helen Peck *85*
drugs *97*
due process *75*
dum-dum bullets *46, 48*
Duncan, Norman *178–179, 179*

E

East Grinstead *87*
East Sussex *9*
Edwards, John *152*
Elva (jury foreperson) *14*
emotion *30*
emotions *193*
empathy *153, 157, 185*
enemies *96, 190*

Ennis, George *179*
Esslemont, Paul *133, 140, 155, 157*
European Court of Human Rights *179*
evidence *71, 172*
    circumstantial evidence *57, 89, 91*
        mild circumstantial evidence *59*
    distressing evidence *135*
    'earth-bound evidence' *177*
    tampering with *178*
experiment *72*
external authority/forces *62, 76*
eye-contact *75*
eye-narrowing *14*

F

Facebook *188*
fair trial *168*
faith *74*
Fletcher, Malcolm *48*
Fletcher, Yvonne *52*
Fogarty, Patrick *14*
footsteps *150, 192*
Forbes, John Gale *71*
Ford Escort/Sierra *96, 147*
forensics *45, 60, 178*
    audio forensics *148*
Forrest, Jeremy *26*
Foster, Det Supt Brian *95*
fraud *65, 108*
freedom of conscience *75*
French, Dr Peter *178*
French, Mr Justice *135, 172*
Fulcher, PC Stephen *86*
Fuld, William *63*
Fuller, Harry *vii, 36*

Arthur Daley character *37*
bankruptcy *38*
claims of celebrity connections *38*
Flash Harry *35–58*
'gipsy romeo', etc. *36*
Harry Fuller's ghost *72*
larger than life *39*
'loveable rogue'/storyteller *38*
time inside *38*
Fuller, Nicola *50, 94, 134, 141, 189*
Fuller, Tom *187*
funeral *50*

G

Gabriel, Colin *180*
gallows humour *140*
gangland *96*
George IV *16*
Gilchrist Solicitors *173*
Gilchrist, Stephen *166, 170, 173*
  bankruptcy petition *175*
Giradet, Peter *182*
Goble's tobacconist *87*
Googling *vii, 187*
Grand Hotel *16*
grass *191*
Greenwood, William and Mitchell *49*
grudge killing *95*
Guess, Gillian *29, 182*
Guildford Four *59*
guns *48, 85, 190*
  gun cupboard *104*
  handguns *48*

H

Hallett, Heather *vii*
Hall, Phil *165*
Harlan, Robert *78*
harmless prank *81*
Hart Fortgang solicitors *173*
Hasbro *65–66*
headlines *167*
Heskett Park *56*
High Court *188*
Hill, Det Ch Supt Graham *96, 147, 190*
Hillsborough Report *82*
holiday camp *19, 139, 156*
Holt, Stephen *178*
Home Office *48, 49, 143*
Home Secretary *60*
Hope, Lord *129*
hotel stays
  tabloid fodder *17*
House of Lords *61, 68, 119, 122, 164*
Hove *16*
  Hove Crown Court *135*
Hubbard, Michael QC *125*
Hungerford *48*
Hynes, Francis *20*

I

'Iceman' *103, 200*
identification *12*
ideomotor *62*
indecency *183*
inferences
  proper inferences *86*
informant *179*
injustice *31*

innocence
  claims of *104*
insurance broking *46*, *56*
internet *187*
IRA *16*, *136*

J

Jekyll and Hyde *191*
Jimerson, Lila *77*
Johnson, Barbara *51*, *142*, *161*
Johnson, Michael *51*, *142*, *158*, *189*
joke *77*
Jones, Gary *163*, *164*
  'Reporter of the Year' *164*
'Judas kiss' *139*
jurors
  absent jurors *72*
  ban on alcohol *150*
  ban on research *187*
  Centre for Jury Studies (USA) *154*
  consensus *35*
  counselling *154*
  debriefing *154*
  deliberations *21*
    ban on investigating *119*
    window into *107–132*
  disclosures illegal *13*
  dismissal from *188*
  drawing lots *116*, *128*
  emotional difficulties *157*
  'empty shells' *145*
  enclosure of *112*
  falling asleep *136*, *183*
  falling in love with barrister *125*
  hotel stays *149*, *156*

  irregularities *111*
  irresponsible jurors *125*
  Juries Act 1974 *17*
  jurors as witnesses *70*
  juror stress *154*
  jury deliberations *78*
  jury nullification *183*
  jury secrecy/'veil' *viii*, *109*, *112*
  letter from a juryperson *9–33*
  manipulation *77*
  mini-jury *58*
  misconduct *29*
  nodding by/to *188*
  Orange jury *21*
  reunion *23*, *157*
  separation *17*, *149*
  sequestering juries *17*
  signalling to *15*, *70*
  texting *130*
  tossing a coin *122*
  world's dumbest jurors *182*

K

Kennard, Charles *62*
Kennard Novelty Company *63*
Kent *96*
Kiszko, Stefan *59–60*, *67*, *83*

L

Lane, Lord Chief Justice Geoffrey *60*
Lawson, Michael QC *25*, *56*, *90*, *111*, *181*
Lawyer, The *166*, *169*
Lee, Roger *97*, *178*
legal aid *173*
  Legal Aid Practitioners Group *173*

Lester, Lord *82*
letter. *See jury/letter from a juryperson*
levity in court *140*
Lewes *9*
   Lewes Crown Court *10, 26*
   Lewes Prison *91*
Libyan embassy shooting *52*
lies *88, 89*
Little Eaton *92*
Lloyds Bank *88*
Lord Chief Justice *11, 24, 163*
   greatest Lord Chief Justice *82*
love letters *189*
Lovell-Pank, Dorian QC *28, 112*
love triangle *55, 95*

M

Maguire Seven *59*
Mansfield, Lord *115*
   Mansfield's window *107–132*
Mansfield, Sir James *117*
Manwaring, Mark *193*
Marchand, Clothilde *77*
material irregularity *67, 70*
Matfield *50*
McComb, John *136*
McConville, Professor Mike *133, 145*
McKay, Simon *192*
McKinnon, Justice Laurie *152*
media *200*
mediums *62*
Mills, Christopher *148*
miscarriage of justice *67, 83, 177, 179, 192*
misconceptions *163*
misconduct *124, 129*

Modern Times *133*
Molseed, Lesley *59*
monomania *72*
Monopoly *65*
Montana *150*
morality *80*
Morgan, Jenny *207*
Morgan, Piers *165*
Mortimer, John QC *184*
motive *55, 89, 94, 96*
murder *vii, 27, 124*

N

Newcastle *76*
News of the World *9, 15, 162*
New Statesman *109*
New Zealand *182, 184*
Nickel, Rachel *177*

O

obsession *72*
Oftel *143*
Ohio *63*
Old Bailey *vii, 134, 170*
Old Ship Hotel, The *10, 15–18*
Operation Arrowhead *94*
opportunity *89*
Ouida *62*
Ouija board
   decline *65*
   German Ouija board case *182*
   glow-in-the-dark Ouija boards *66*
   'Goodbye', etc. *57*
   makeshift Ouija board *35*
   marketing *64, 81*

meaning *61*
origin of name *61*
Ouija board apps *66*
Ouija board underwear *66*

P

Paganini, Niccolò *16*
panic *94*
Parents of Murdered Children *193*
Parker Brothers *65, 81*
parlour game *65*
partiality *141*
pathology *52*
Peck, Helen Dow *71*
Pembury *55, 92, 193*
  Pembury Players *161*
Penry-Davey, David QC *24, 111, 168, 173, 174*
Perrigo, Debbie *151*
perverting the course of justice *29*
police
  Sussex Police *86, 87, 91*
Pople, Alison *177*
Porsche *37, 87, 92*
prayer *76*
prejudice *82, 152, 169, 170*
prime suspect
  suspect *45*
Priory Clinic *174*
protection *92*
Provincial Insurance Company *57*
Pryce, Vicky *107*
psychology *65, 76*
psychopathy *168*
publicity *139*

Q

Queen's Bench *136*

R

racism *121, 189*
Ramé, Maria Louise *62*
reconstruction *45, 54, 96, 147, 192*
recorded phone message *135*
re-trial *82, 113, 170*
reward *96*
risk *31, 65, 170*
Roberts, Paul *208*
Rollock Ashley *123*
Routley, Ann *157*
Royal Commission *60, 67, 164*
Rozenberg, Joshua *138*
Rumpole of the Bailey *184*
R v Hynes *20*
R v Young *vii, 61*
Ryan, Michael *48*

S

scoop *165*
séance *vii, 61, 72*
secretiveness *30*
security camera *88*
Sellafield *136*
shady dealings *54*
Shaughnessy, Alison *139*
shock *86, 162*
silence
  right to silence *86*
  silencing a witness *58*
Simpson, O J *154*
Slapper, Professor Gary *74, 183*

Smile of a Killer *89*
smuggling *16*
Snelling, Det Ch Insp Alan *54, 95, 148*
social media *188*
Solicitors' Complaints Bureau *174*
sources *201*
speaking with the dead *153*
speculation *11*
Spencer, Professor John *105, 120*
spirit communication *65*
spiritualism *62*
split personality *190*
Stagg, Colin *177*
star signs *76*
Steyn, Lord *127*
Strange, Sir John *115*
Strangeways riot *134*
stress *154*
stupidity *187*
Sturman, Jim QC *177*
subconscious *35, 65*
Sudoku *182*
supernatural *77*
superstition *74*
Supreme Court *144*
Supreme Court (USA) *65*
surveillance *91*

T

table-turning *62*
tabloids
   cash payments by *186*
tape-recording *145*
Taylor, Peter QC/Lord Chief Justice *11, 59, 67, 110, 134, 155*

telepathy *71*
Tettersell, Nicholas *16*
Thackeray, William Makepeace *16*
Thatcher, Margaret *16, 82*
Thorpe, Jeremy *109*
threats *173*
timings *145*
Tottenham Three *59*
transcripts *200*
Treasury Solicitor *28, 68, 70, 81, 200*
Trivial Pursuit *65*
Tunbridge Wells *40, 50*
   Tunbridge Wells Library *200*
   Tunbridge Wells Police Station *96*
two person theory *191*
tyre expert *189*

U

unconscious *62, 65*
Uplands Community College *41, 148*
Utah *75, 76*

V

Vancouver *29*
Vanity Fair *16*
Vezey v Delaval *116*
victims *145, 162, 186, 189, 193*
   'channelling the victim' *152*
   life sentence *162*
   victimisation *65*
   Victims of Crime Trust *193*
video *88*
violence *103*
VW Golf *88*

W

Waco, Texas *148*
Waddington, David QC *60*, *67*
Wadhurst *40*, *51*, *87*
  'Miss Marple village' *40*
  Wadhurst History Society *200*, *208*
Walther PPK *92*, *174*
Waterhouse, Sir Ronald *70*
Waters, Colin *174*
weapons
  Young's arsenal *89*
Weekly World News *182*
West, Iain *52*
West, Rosemary *154*
West Yorkshire police *83*
whispering *192*
whistleblower *185*
Widgery, Lord *110*
wig *47*
Wormwood Scrubs *167*, *174*

Y

Yorkshire Ripper *134*
Young and Harding Associates *56*, *92*
Young, Stephen *vii*
  changing story *89*
  character *173*
  dark side *190*
  debts *57*, *89*, *103*, *181*, *190*
  'Mr Cool' *103*
  remanded in custody *50*
  TV appearance from prison *161*
  well-liked *103*
YouTube *107*, *108*, *129*

217

Other books about the jury from Waterside Press...

The Criminal Jury Old and New
*Jury Power from Early Times
to the Present Day*
by John Hostettler

Ballot Box to Jury Box
*The Life and Times of an
English Crown Court Judge*
by John Baker

A first-rate account of the jury—from its genesis to the present day. This book deals with all the great political and legal landmarks and shows how the jury developed—and survived to become a key democratic institution capable of resisting monarchs, governments and sometimes plain law. Linking past and present, John Hostettler conveys the unique nature of the jury, and its central role in the administration of justice—but above all its importance as 'a thing of the people' and a barrier to manipulation and abuse of power.

Paperback & eBook | ISBN 978-1-904380-11-5
2004 | 168 pages

This candid and often humorous autobiography traces John Baker's political ambitions and tells how he came to discard the ballot box for the court bench, of his experiences as a politician, broadcaster, lawyer, judge and family man, and the array of leading lights and everyday folk whom he met in the course of twin careers spanning over half a century.

'Entertaining ... this is an engaging account of a fascinating man'
— *The Times*

Paperback & eBook | ISBN 978-1-904380-19-1
2005 | 210 pages

… and see more at www.WatersidePress.co.uk

Thomas Erskine and Trial by Jury
by John Hostettler

Thomas Erskine (1750-1823) was one of the greatest advocates ever to appear in an English court of law. As King's Counsel he was involved in many celebrated trials, including the prosecution of John Horne Took for seditious libel and of Queen Caroline for adultery. His other notable achievements include the successful defence of Thomas Paine's *Rights of Man*, which cost him the post of Attorney-General to the Prince of Wales. He also served as MP for Portsmouth and for just one year as Lord Chancellor. Latterly the First Baron Erskine, this book covers his controversial career and rise to high office.

Paperback & eBook | ISBN 978-1-904380-59-7
2010 | 272 pages

Sir William Garrow
His Life, Times and Fight for Justice
by John Hostettler and Richard Braby. With a Foreword by Geoffrey Robertson QC

Garrow's 'gifts to the world' include altering the relationship between judge and jury (the former had until then dominated over the latter in criminal trials), helping to forge the presumption of innocence and ensuring a general right to put forward a defence using a trained lawyer.

'Without the pioneering work of William Garrow, the legal system would be stuck in the Middle Ages'
— *Radio Times*

Paperback & eBook | ISBN 978-1-904380-69-6
2011 | 352 pages